The Green Kitchen

The Green Kitchen

Delicious and Healthy Vegetarian Recipes for Every Day

David Frenkiel & Luise Vindahl

Contents

Introduction

The moment we met, our two food worlds collided.
I was the unhealthy vegetarian (yes, they do exist) who
basically lived on pasta, pizza, sweets and ice cream.
And Luise was a very health-conscious meat eater,
who had practically scratched those foods from her
repertoire. After a couple of awkward months (huge
understatement), we made a decision. We realized that
if we were to be able to live together, I had to learn
about wholegrains, quinoa and natural sweeteners,
while Luise decided to start cutting down on meat
and start experimenting with vegetable-based meals.
And instead of focusing on all the things we didn't eat,
we did the opposite.

All of a sudden we found ourselves discussing how
to cook a dinner that put the vegetables in focus, and
was still nourishing enough to eat after a long day or a
workout. We filled our home with fruit, vegetables, nuts,
seeds, wholegrains and good fats and decided to start
cooking food and baking cakes that were healthy and
green, without being boring.

One of the first things we made was a carrot cake,
where you could actually feel the texture and taste of
the carrots, not just the sugar in it. And we made baked
herb falafel that we wrapped in thin, crunchy cabbage
leaves instead of plain, dry pitta bread. We also learned to
appreciate simple things like a freshly squeezed vegetable
juice, which tastes sweeter than anything you can buy
in the supermarket, yet contains no sugar at all. The
possibilities seemed endless and everything we made
tasted so much better than it had ever done before.
As a way of documenting our food endeavours (and
failures) we bought a camera, registered the blog

Green Kitchen Stories, and started writing. And that is what we have been doing for more than three years now. This book is a resume of what we have learned and perhaps a guide, of sorts, to our way of eating.

To help you get the full picture, we will rewind the tape a couple of years. Our story started late one night on a small dance floor not more than 10 meters from the river Tiber and 20 meters from Castel Sant'Angelo, in central Rome. That is where we met and fell in love six years ago. I don't think the subject of food came up once during our first conversation (strange considering that we were in Italy and everybody ALWAYS talks about food there). But I know for a fact that we talked about it on our first date one week later. I was so nervous that I memorised 20 questions, to avoid having nothing to say. And after having lived in Rome for six months, 15 of those questions were food-related. It didn't take us long to realise that we had two vastly different approaches to food.

I have been a vegetarian since I was 15 years old. It has never been a radical choice for me. I am not a meat-hater. I have just chosen to eat vegetables instead. It makes me feel better in every way possible. I can sit around a table with people eating steaks, without commenting or even thinking about it. But I do expect the same treatment back. What I eat is my choice; please spare me any ironic comments. Although I enjoyed spending time in the kitchen before I met Luise, the largest part of my plate was always filled with pasta, potatoes, bread and white rice.

Luise has always been a cautious eater. She makes lots of deliberately healthy choices that for some might seem complicated, but for her makes perfect sense. She has always had an active lifestyle, and eating well is an essential part of that. She eats some fish and organic poultry occasionally, but has become amazingly creative in turning a few vegetables into a feast. For her, health is not only about eating green, she is also very interested in herbal medicine and natural remedies. And she obviously must be doing something right, because I have never met a person who looks so healthy and recovers so quickly from a virus.

Today we live in a crammed but charming apartment in Stockholm, Sweden, with our daughter, Elsa. Although we both have careers of our own, and none of us have any professional background in cooking, food has become something we talk about from early morning to late evening.

We try to eat as varied a diet as possible at home. That is why our recipes are sometimes raw and other times cooked. Sometimes they call for buckwheat, which is gluten-free and other times for spelt, which is not. Many of our recipes are vegan, but we love to eat eggs and cheese every now and then. Look into our kitchen and you will not only notice all the nuts that Elsa has spread over the floor, but also the wide array of whole flours, dried fruit, seeds, superfoods and multi-coloured quinoa that we keep in our cupboard. Open our fridge and you will probably be attacked by an organic and locally harvested cabbage. It's usually so big that we throw it in just before closing the door, thus it is also the first thing that jumps out when you open it. Behind it you might find some more seasonal vegetables (organic, when not too expensive), seven million jars of nut butters and spreads, a goat's yoghurt and three different versions of plant milk, usually oat, almond and rice. Even though it might sound like a parody, this is an exact description of how our kitchen looks right now. We don't have a perfect and clean home, but we do love whole foods.

This book is filled with recipes from our everyday life, along with some simple tips on how to get a more varied and greener pantry. We want to keep it simple, basic and very useful. Here we have shared the kind of food that we often eat at home. Not all our recipes can be whipped together in 20 minutes, but many of them can (a few in even less time). Some of them will take hours, but they are worth it. We have tried to make sure that there will be lots of recipes to choose from (or adapt) if you are vegan or have any allergies. More than 90 per cent of the recipes in this book are, by the way, gluten-free.

We have divided the book into Mornings (where you will find breakfasts both for a stressful Tuesday and a weekend brunch); Lighter Meals (suitable for lunches and effortless dinners throughout the week); Good to Go (dishes that will survive a few hours in a picnic basket); Family Dinners (perfect for a larger weekend gatherings); Small Bites (for a buffet table or as a side dish); Drinks (from fresh juices to Indian chai tea); and Sweets & Treats (to trigger your sweet tooth, even though naturally sweetened with fruit and full of wholegrains).

We find food inspiration from all over the globe. Of course we read a lot of blogs, but our little family has also travelled around the world together. You can probably trace which countries we have visited, just by looking at the recipe index. One country that we always return to is Italy, and you will definitely notice the influence in how we use oil, lemon and fresh herbs. Apart from that, we have also thrown a little bit of our Scandinavian heritage into this book. A classic dark Danish rye bread, a Swedish hash pan, a cold Danish berry soup, a curried egg salad, a mouth-watering pancake cake and delicious thin crisp bread. We have included recipes that most Scandinavian families have their own versions of, but with our own twist. Most of the recipes are written solely for this book, but we have also included our favourites from the blog. They have new photos and many of them have also been altered in different ways – new flavours have been added, the methods have been perfected or there are new suggestions of what to serve them with. So even though you might recognise a recipe, it might be worth trying it again.

Luise and I have written this book and developed all the recipes together. Both our voices will guide you through it (and sometimes also the voice of our daughter). We hope that you will find many new favourite recipes, but also that we can inspire you to pursue your own way into the world of whole foods.

5

Inside Our Pantry

Although the ingredients we have in our kitchen are constantly shifting, there are a large number of items that we make sure to keep in stock. Here we have organised them in lists, with short explanations of each product – see this as our guide how to make our Green Kitchen move in to yours. With these ingredients at home, you will not only be ready to try most of the recipes in this book, but also ready to start improvising yourself. Changing towards a greener, healthier and more versatile storecupboard really makes a difference in helping to improve your eating habits. It will be so much easier baking with natural sweeteners or whole grains once you have them to hand. It is unfortunately quite costly to buy organic products, whole grains, nuts and seeds, so don't feel obliged to get all of them at once, just make sure you have a few ingredients in each category.

BUTTER, VINEGAR AND OIL

Being on the healthy track doesn't mean avoiding fat, quite the opposite. It is highly important. But of course it matters what kind of oils and fats you choose, which you heat and which you use raw. Here are our favourites.

Butter

Adds great taste to cookies and sweets. We sometimes replace it with the more neutral coconut oil. Choose organic butter from grass-fed cows if you can.

Ghee (clarified butter)

Very delicious raw, but also perfect for frying because of its high smoking point. Use for both sweet and savoury food. To make Ghee see the recipe on page 25.

Apple cider vinegar

Our favourite vinegar, it has a fruity and sour taste and is cheaper than many other vinegars. Great in salad dressings.

Balsamic vinegar

A dark vinegar with a rich smooth, sweet and sour taste

Red and white wine vinegar

Perfect in salads and marinades.

Rice vinegar

Good in Asian food and, of course, rice. We use it in our Sushi Explosion on page 132.

Cold-pressed flax oil

High in omega-3 and -6, which are important for vegans. We mainly use it in smoothies.

Extra-virgin coconut oil/butter

Sold with or without coconut flavour. It has a high smoking point, so is ideal for frying. Liquid or 'creamy' at room temperature and solid when kept in the fridge. We often use it in raw desserts.

Extra-virgin olive oil

Best used raw or heated at low temperatures. We use stronger flavoured olive oil in salads or drizzled over our pizza, and milder for frying and baking.

Extra-virgin rapeseed oil

Very common in Scandinavia. Has a nice nutty taste and is perfect as it is or in baked goods.

Unrefined sesame oil

A very flavoursome oil, you often need only a few drops. Good in Asian food. We use it for marinating tofu, in salads and noodle dishes.

NUTS AND SEEDS

Look inside our pantry and you will find an almost frightening amount of nuts and seeds. We are true addicts and use them in everything from breakfasts, salads, dinners and desserts. They are rich in proteins, good fats and minerals, and therefore very important in a vegetarian diet.

Almonds

Contain a high amount of good fat. Can be turned into nut butter easily. We use them toasted in salads, granola and desserts.

Amaranth

An even smaller gluten-free seed than quinoa, but slightly higher in protein. We have stuffed tomatoes with cooked amaranth on page 152.

Brazil nuts

We love them soaked as a snack or in our Breakfast Blend on page 46.

Cashew nuts

A sweet and rich nut. Good for soaking and making raw cream or raw cheese.

Desiccated and flaked coconut

Good in breakfasts, baking, smoothies and soups.

Hazelnuts

Great with both sweet and savoury food. Try the Hazelnut, Aubergine & Mushroom Parcels on page 126.

Hemp seeds

Although this seed is a relative of Marijuana, it doesn't get you high. It has a nutty, almost sweet taste and is packed with protein and a wide variety of minerals and vitamins. Makes good plant milk, but even better as a raw topping on muesli.

Hulled buckwheat

A gluten-free, 3-d triangular seed. We use it in our Buckwheat & Ginger Porridge on page 57.

Linseeds (Flax seeds)

Brown or golden, rich in omega-3 fatty acid. We add to desserts, bread and smoothies to make them more nutritious.

Macadamia nuts

Crispy white nuts. Delicious as they are and in chocolate desserts.

Nut and seed butters

Perfect as a bread spread, on porridge, in smoothies and in raw chocolate mousse. We usually keep several different varieties at home. Our favourites are peanut, tahini (sesame), almond, sunflower and apricot kernel.

Pine nuts

Expensive little nuts and pesto's best friend.

Pistachio nuts

Not only our favourite ice cream flavour, also wonderful in muffins and in savoury food together with goat's cheese.

Psyllium seeds

Good in gluten-free baking. They bind moisture and help make bread less crumbly.

Pumpkin seeds

This seed that adds an extra dimension to everything from granola to soups and salads. They have a slight grainy texture when raw, crunchy when roasted.

Quinoa (red, white and black)

A gluten-free super-seed, packed with protein and fibre. Different colours have slightly different tastes. Beautiful in salads.

Sunflower seeds

Contain less fat than nuts and are less allergenic. David's favourite seed – he uses it a lot in baking and desserts. We often give them a quick roast to enhance the flavour. Check out the crust on our Frozen Strawberry Cheesecake on page 218.

Walnuts

Same shape as a brain and that is exactly what they are good for. Good in baking.

DRIED BEANS, LENTILS AND PEAS

Pulses are the vegetarian's number one source of protein. They are rich in fibre and high in minerals, vitamins and complex carbohydrates, and are a really cheap source of protein. Buy large bags of dried beans, peas and lentils, soak, cook and freeze in portions and you'll always have an easy meal at hand. Cooking instructions on page 28.

Adzuki beans

These flavourful small beans are also known as the 'weight loss bean'. They are good in 'chilli sin carne' or other bean stews.

Beluga and Puy lentils

Beautiful looking and wonderful flavours. Hold together better than red and yellow lentils. We serve them as an alternative to rice and pasta.

Black beans

Most common bean in Latin American cooking. Try our Savoy Tacos on page 82.

Black/yellow-eyed beans

Cream-coloured beans with a characteristic black or

yellow spot 'eye'. Dressed lightly in olive oil, lemon and herbs, they make a delicious salad.

Borlotti beans
If you have the opportunity to get these beans fresh, they are incredibly beautiful. Great in soups.

Butter (Lima) beans
Large white bean, perfect in a mixed bean salad and they add a silky creaminess to soups.

Cannellini beans
Small white bean. Good as a spread on bread or in our bean version of a risotto on page 146.

Chickpeas (Garbanzos)
Elsa's favourite. Leave a bowl of boiled chickpeas in front of her, and they will be gone within minutes. We use them in salads, soups and hummus.

Haricot (navy) beans
This small white bean has a sweet flavour and can be used as an alternative to cannellini beans.

Kidney beans
Kidney-shaped, of course, and sweet in taste. Great in spicy stews.

Mung beans
Beautiful colour and Luise's favourite sprouting bean. Try the sprouted mung bean Sprout Ceviche on page 167.

Pinto beans
Pinto means 'painted' in Spanish which is what they look like. We use them as a bruschetta topping.

Red, yellow and green lentils
Great in soups and in Indian food. Try our Sweet Apricot & Cauliflower Dal on page 115.

Tofu
Made from soy beans. Nice warm or cold and perfect for making a dish more filling. Choose organic non-GMO if possible.

Yellow and green split peas
Sweeter and creamier than lentils. Try our Rhubarb, Apple & Yellow Split Pea Stew on page 116.

PLANT-BASED MILK AND CREAM

The milk debate has been hot in the last couple of years and a lot has been said for and against, so let's not bore you more with that. Instead we have listed our favourite milks and creams. Most can be used as a straight substitute for dairy milk but use soy or coconut milk if you need to heat it. There are many good kinds to try so start the tasting.

Coconut milk
A natural fat plant milk. Used commonly in Indian stews, but we also use it in desserts, ice creams and shakes.

Goat's milk
Thick and creamy and usually available from small farms, although some supermarkets and health food stores do stock it.

Hemp milk
Homemade sweetened hemp milk is much better than store-bought, which can be a little bitter.

Nut milk
Make your own, by following our recipe on page 27.

Oat cream, soya cream and nut cream
Great non-dairy alternatives to regular cream. Buy in-store or see our recipe on page 27.

Oat milk
The one we most often keep at home, because it's easy to get in Sweden and less expensive than, for example, almond milk. If you can't find any, make your own by following our recipe on page 27.

Rice milk
We use it in smoothies, it is a bit sweeter than oat milk.

Soya milk
Great for heating and making foam.

NATURAL SWEETENERS

Whether you look at recipe for an indulgent dessert, a decadent cake or a sweet drink you won't find sugar anywhere in this book (apart from in the recipe to make your own Bubbling Kombucha Cocktail on page 184). A few years ago we started moving to more natural alternatives to sweeten our recipes. Today we don't even keep regular sugar at home. It was a challenge for us in the beginning but now we really appreciate the natural flavours that come with these sweeteners.

Apple syrup, juice and unsweetened sauce
Pure apples that are pressed into a juice and boiled down to a syrup are great in fruit juices, granolas and baking, but also in marinades. Apple sauce can be used as a sweetener or to replace eggs in cakes. Both are easy to make at home. See page 30.

Bananas
Use to sweeten shakes and smoothies, but also fruitier cakes. Can be substituted with very ripe pears.

Birch sugar (natural xylitol)
Dissolves quickly and looks and tastes similar to sugar. Only use small amounts. We mix it with cinnamon and drizzle over rice porridge.

Coconut palm sugar
Looks very similar to granulated sugar, it has a caramel-like taste and is great in cookies.

Dried unsulphured apricots and prunes
Truly good sweeteners in stews, compotes, porridge and jam.

Fresh and dried dates, and date syrup (molasses)
Very sweet. Good to mix with nuts into delicious vegan cakes, crusts and truffles. Raw Date Syrup (see page 30) is a great substitute for agave, honey, maple syrup and yacon syrup.

Pure maple syrup
When Elsa was born, a blog reader sent us a bottle of pure maple syrup from Canada and we have been in love with it ever since. We use it in baking, on pancakes, waffles, porridge or oatmeal.

Raw honey and clear honey
We are so lucky to have friends who provide us with delicious raw honey. Honey contains antioxidants, minerals and vitamins and is therefore a great natural sweetener. Try a morning shot – add it to hot water, honey, ginger, lemon and ghee.

Vanilla extract, vanilla beans or ground vanilla
We love vanilla. It gives desserts a sweet and characteristic touch.

PASTA AND NOODLES

There are many more nutritious and flavourful varieties than the traditional wheat noodle. They come in many colours, tastes and shapes.

Kelp noodles
A sea vegetable made into raw noodles. Neutral in flavour. Easy to dress up in a tasty dressing.

Udon rice, and soba buckwheat noodles
Good gluten-free varieties. Great in Asian salads or spicy coconut soups.

Wholegrain and gluten-free pasta
Available in many varieties like corn, spelt, buckwheat and rice.

Wholegrain lasagne
We often use courgette, sweet potato or aubergine slices instead, but when we don't, we use wholegrain lasagne.

FLOURS AND GRAINS

When we started using wholewheat flour instead of white plain (all-purpose) flour, it was because it left us with healthier bread and desserts. But after learning more about the different qualities, textures and flavours of each flour we realised that we now bake more flavoursome and interesting cakes, bread and pancakes than we ever did before. Many of our flours are gluten-free, but not all of them.

Almond flour

Gluten-free and wonderful to use in pie and tart cases. Adds a sweet nuttiness to everything. Make it yourself by simply grinding raw almonds into a fine powdered flour, or buy ready-made.

Baking powder and baking soda

Essential in muffins, scones and all baked goods that don't call for leavening.

Brown rice flour

A gluten-free flour with a nutty flavour. Good in baking. We often use it combined with other flours.

Buckwheat flour

Gluten-free with an earthy flavour. We use to make pancakes and crepes, but it is also good in muffins.

Chestnut flour

Gluten-free. Available from most health food stores. It has an incredibly nutty flavour and is good in crepes, breads and cakes.

Chickpea (Barbanzo/Besan) flour

One of our favourite gluten-free flours. Good mixed with almond flour in pie and tart cases, and also for making pancakes.

Cornflour (Cornstarch)

Fine-ground, white powdered maize used for thickening and baking.

Cornmeal

Gluten-free with a distinct corn taste. Great for making tortillas, cornbread or our savoury muffins on page 95.

Kamut flour

Kamut is a nutritious whole grain in the wheat family. It is a better alternative than normal wheat flour.

Quinoa flour

Gluten-free and rich in protein. Makes moist baked goods.

Rye flour

Dark grain that we use in rye bread, pancake batters, cookies and crispbread. Not very elastic and difficult to knead, therefore more suited to looser batters and doughs.

Spelt flour

Ancient cousin to wheat. Less refined, with more fibres and less gluten (although not gluten-free). Mild and sweet flavour, it is our favourite flour to bake with. Good elasticity and leavening. Don't knead it too long, or it can become crumbly.

Wheatgerm

A powerhouse of nutrition. You can replace one half to one cup of the flour in baking. Use it in pancakes, waffles, bread and cookies.

Fresh and dried active yeast

Most of our bread and pizza recipes use dried yeast because we always have it at home. But you can use fresh yeast instead. Follow instructions on the packet for use.

Arrowroot

A natural starch. Use in baking, and to thicken stews, desserts and soups. Don't continue to cook after it thickens or it goes runny again. We use it in our Beet Bourguignon recipe on page 121.

Millet

Gluten-free and rich in fibre and protein. We use it as a gluten-free couscous replacer or mash it together with cauliflower for a side dish.

Polenta

Gluten-free coarse-ground cornmeal. Use to accompany a dinner instead of mashed potato.

Can also be cooked with cinnamon and nut milk for a sweet version.

Rice – red, black, wild, brown

Gluten-free. The varieties of colours, flavours and textures are amazing and so much healthier than refined white rice. Wild rice is actually a grass.

Rolled oats

Use in baked oatmeal and crunchy cookies. Can be used as an egg-free binder in veggie burgers and polpette. Many oats have traces of gluten, but you can buy gluten-free rolled oats.

Rye berry, wheat berry, spelt berry and barley

Come as entire kernels (without the husk). Soak and cook with herbs or spices and they'll make your salad into a feast. Good in stews and in bread too. Try the Dark Danish Rye Bread on page 58.

Wholegrain couscous

Wheat grain, often served with north African dishes and good in salads. Try with our Moroccan Vegetable Tagine on page 125.

SUPERFOODS

We use these products to add nutrition to smoothies, desserts or baked goods. They'll give your body a concentrated amount of high nutrients. Some of these might be very expensive and others quite cheap, depending on where in the world you live, so go and have a look in your local health food store.

Acai powder

Beautiful purple berry from South America. Contains more antioxidants than blueberries. Only sold frozen or dried and can be difficult to find. We mostly use it in smoothies or blends.

Bee pollen

Small yellow/orange granules. Naturally good together with honey. Sweet tasting. Perfect in smoothies. Looks pretty when sprinkled over porridge and desserts.

Carob powder

Looks similar to cacao and is good to combine with it. The taste is slightly different, but still sweet. Rich in calcium. We add it to chocolate mousse or use in baking.

Chia seeds

A power seed even more nutritious than linseeds (flaxseeds), but also more expensive. We often use it as an egg substitute in baking, or in our smoothies.

Dried goji, inca, mulberries, cranberries

Antioxidant-rich super berries, choose organic if possible.

Dried nettles

Packed with iron. Buy in health food stores or hang fresh nettles up until dry and then crush them by hand. We use in smoothies, porridge, pancakes, bread and tea.

Hemp, pea or brown rice protein powder

Nutritious natural protein powders, great in your morning smoothie or post-workout drink. Also great for children's 'I-refuse-to-eat' phases.

Nori sheets

Seaweed made from the red algae. We use when making sushi, nori rolls and sushi salad. To be honest, this is the only algae we are crazy about.

Raw cacao powder and nibs

High quality superfood. High in magnesium and very rich in antioxidants. Great in raw desserts.

Rosehip powder

Made from dried rosehip. Very high in vitamin C.

Tastes like fruit and flowers. We love it in baked cakes, bread, but also on our morning yoghurt.

Spirulina powder

A blue-green micro algae. Add a spoonful in drinks or make the Spirulina Chocolate Truffles on page 232.

Wheatgrass powder

Very healthy. Often used in holistic medicine for regenerating cells. We often mix it with lemon to neutralise the flavour. Try our Green Cleanse Power Shot on page 193.

FERMENTED ESSENTIALS

Fermented food contains natural probiotic (a type of living bacteria), which is the key of our overall health and wellbeing. It is the best medicine for the digestive system.

Kimchi

Fermented Chinese cabbage with lots of chilli. We use it in stews to get an Asian twist. David makes his own, but you can buy it in Asian stores.

Kombucha

Fermented bubbling tea. We always keep a kombucha mushroom ready in a jar. See page 184.

Miso

Asian paste made from fermented beans or grains. Use it in soups, spreads or sauces. Not all miso pastes are vegetarian. Choose organic and non-GMO if you can get it.

Sauerkraut

Lacto-fermented white cabbage. Super-healthy and perfect for a topping on stews or as a sandwich filling.

Sourdough

Natural leavening and lactic acid fermentation is why sourdough makes the most healthy bread you can find. Good with rye flour.

Soy sauce and tamari

Asian sauce made from fermented bean or grain paste, choose organic and non-GMO if possible.

KITCHEN APPLIANCES

Our kitchen has limited space, so we have only invested in a few appliances that we can use for almost everything. For example, we don't have a bread-making machine which is why the instructions in all our bread recipes are by hand. If using a machine you can of course skip the kneading.

Blender

After working our way through a couple of cheaper brands we finally bought a Vitamix. It is one of the most powerful blenders on the market and can easily puree nuts into perfectly smooth nut butter or nut milk, and make all smoothies thick and creamy.

Hand (immersion) blender and food processor

Our most used kitchen machine. Although I had a pretty nasty accident with this, we still use it almost every day. We use the hand blender for soups and smoothies and then connect it to a food processor that we use to make pesto and grind nuts.

Juice machine

Although a hassle to clean, we use our juice machine surprisingly often to turn week-old vegetables and fruit into sweet juice, instead of throwing them away. Turn to page 188 for juicing tips.

Kitchen scales

Scales are the only way to make sure that the measurements are correct when baking. Digital works best, since you can reset to use with different containers.

Pestle and mortar

Great for grinding spices and making pestos. Freshly ground spices taste more intense than store-bought.

Healthy Start

When Elsa was born, food became even more important to us. We knew from the start that we wanted her to eat the same things we did. When starting to plan this book, we discussed including a chapter with children's food, but as we twisted and turned the subject, we realized that from the moment Elsa started eating solid food, she has actually been given the same things that we eat. And it has worked, so instead of sharing special children's recipes, we'll just give you our best tips on how to give your kids a good and healthy start to eating well. These things have worked for us and for Elsa, hopefully they will be helpful for you too.

Start as you mean to go on . . .

Try to reduce or eliminate gluten and dairy products during your baby's first year or two. They can be hard to digest for anyone, but especially for young children. Even if they have no allergies or food intolerances, many people react to these food irritants. No sugar during your baby's first years. Sugar tastes good but has lots of downsides – it causes hyperactivity, lowers the immune system and can lead to tooth decay, to mention a few. We also have our own personal theory about sugar: once you start offering sweets, it will be harder to get children to try things that are not sweet. The longer you prolong the introduction of sugar, the more your children will be open to trying new foods and eating their greens, which makes life a whole lot easier for you.

'One ice-cream every now and then won't hurt her'. You wouldn't believe how many times we've heard that sentence. And sure, they are right, she eats an ice cream and life goes on. But why? Until she was two years old, Elsa never asked for ice cream herself, she didn't even know what it was. During a child's first two years we as adults choose what food our children should eat and they learn from this – it's our responsibility. If someone wants to give your baby an ice cream, it's probably not because your baby asks for it, it's because they want to give it to her. It's worth thinking about.

If you are vegetarian, we recommend that you raise your children to be the same until they are old enough to express their own opinion. Why give your child something that you wouldn't eat yourself? They will get plenty of proteins, fats, vitamins and minerals from vegetables, eggs, cheese, oils, fruit, beans, lentils, seeds and nuts. You can also give them a vitamin and mineral supplement for small children.

EIGHT TIPS ON HOW TO GIVE YOUR CHILDREN A HEALTHY START IN LIFE:

1. AGREE

Talk everything through with your partner so you both agree on why you are doing this. If you don't agree, every dinner will be an issue. Also discuss with your families and close friends to help them out with food suggestions. Otherwise, they might not dare invite you or your child for dinner any more ...

2. KEEP IT SIMPLE

Don't change your and your child's eating habits to the impossible. Find a level that you and your family can live with. We decided that Elsa could eat fish when she stays with other families or in day care, even though we don't eat it at home. It makes life easier for them, plus she get lots of good fats and proteins from it.

3. BE A GOOD ROLE MODEL

The most important thing is not what food you put in front of your children, but what you eat yourself. That is what your children will want to eat as well. We rarely make special food for Elsa and we would never eat an ice cream in front of her if we weren't prepared to give her one too.

4. EXPERIMENT WITH SHAPE & TEXTURE

If a child does not like a certain food, try to cook it in different ways. It is not always the taste that children don't like, but sometimes the shape or texture.

5. BOOST THEIR FAVOURITE FOOD

A simple trick to get extra minerals and vitamins in your children's diet is to add superfood ingredients to their favourite foods. Add vegetable juice, for example, when making bread or muffins. Blend spinach in pancake batter or broccoli, nettle powder or linseeds in berry smoothies and porridge (they won't taste it).

6. ALWAYS HAVE A SNACK TO HAND

A difficulty with healthy eating habits is when your children see other children eating something and they want the same. It can be anything from a hot dog to sweets. We learned early on to always carry a snack or fruit with us, so we can offer her that instead. If you look into Elsa's backpack you will probably always find a hard boiled egg, a carrot, a piece of fruit or some Quinoa, Cauliflower & Ramsons Cakes (see page 71).

7. KEEP CALM

If you see your child with a cookie, don't get hysterical and grab it from them as it will have the opposite effect. It's only food and it is important to develop a natural relationship with unhealthy food too.

8. ENCOURAGE EATING

We have been very laid-back about table manners. As long as she eats, we don't mind if it's with a fork, a spoon, a chopstick, a straw or her hands (soup can get pretty messy). The good part is that she eats (almost) anything that we put in front of her. If you set up too many rules around eating you will probably end up with a food strike.

HEALTHY START

Basic Methods

We have listed a few basic recipes and methods here for things that we often do ourselves. Everything from a simple tomato sauce, which you will have use for in many of the savoury recipes in this book, to how to make a simple date syrup that can be used to replace other syrups, honey and molasses in most recipes. You can buy most of these foods at supermarkets or health food stores, and we do that ourselves from time to time, but by making them yourself you get to decide what to put in them.

VEGETABLE STOCK
Makes about 3.5 litres (6 pints/15 cups)

2 tbsp extra virgin olive oil
2 onions, quartered, unpeeled
3 garlic cloves, unpeeled
2 carrots, chopped
2 leeks, chopped
1 fennel bulb, chopped
1 celery stick, chopped
10–20 flat-leaf parsley stems
4 bay leaves
5 black or white peppercorns
2 tsp sea salt

Heat the oil in a stockpot on a medium heat. Add the onions, garlic, carrots, leeks, fennel and celery. Sauté for 3–5 minutes until lightly browned and soft. Add the parsley, bay leaves, pepper, salt and 4 litres (7 pints/16 cups) water. Bring to a boil, then lower the heat to very low, cover and gently simmer for about 1 hour or longer if you have time. Taste and adjust seasoning if necessary. Strain the stock and leave to cool, stirring occasionally. Measure out 250 ml (8½ fl oz/1 cup) or 450 ml (15 fl oz/2 cups) portions and keep in containers in the freezer for up to 6 months. Keeps in the fridge for 1 week.

BASIC TOMATO SAUCE
Makes around 1 litre (34 fl oz/4 cups)

2 tbsp extra virgin olive oil
1 yellow onion, finely chopped
2 garlic cloves, finely chopped
½ tsp dried chilli
3 x 400 g (14 oz) cans whole plum tomatoes
5 sprigs of basil, leaves picked
sea salt
freshly ground black pepper

Heat the olive oil in a saucepan on a medium heat. Add the onion, garlic and chilli and sauté for a couple of minutes until golden. Stir in the tomatoes, basil, salt and pepper. Use a wooden spoon to crush the tomatoes. Lower the heat, cover and gently simmer for about 20 minutes. Use immediately or cool and store in an air-tight glass jar in the fridge (keeps for about one week).

BASIC METHODS

GHEE (CLARIFIED BUTTER)
Makes 1 jar

500 g (1 lb/2 oz) unsalted butter

You will also need:
1 piece of cheesecloth/muslin or a sieve
1 airtight, heatproof glass jar

Heat the butter in a heavy-based saucepan over a medium heat until it has melted. Do not cover the pan. Lower the heat as much as possible and let gently simmer until foam rises to the top of the melted butter. The butter will make lots of spluttering, which means that the butter is boiling, and 3 layers will develop: a white top layer, a liquid yellow layer, and a milk solids bottom layer. This takes about 15–20 minutes. Stir every now and then with a wooden spoon to keep the solids from sticking to the bottom. When the butter is done it will smell like freshly baked croissants and turn to a clear golden yellow colour with a little white foam floating on top. Remove from the heat immediately or it will burn.
Place a few layers of cloth or a sieve over the glass jar and carefully pour the hot liquid butter through into the glass. Leave to cool and solidify before closing the airtight lid. Store in the fridge for up to one year, or at room temperature for 3 months.

Tip: You can use all kind of herbs and spices to flavour or colour your ghee. Add when the butter is melted and leave it until the end of the process. Try garlic, ginger, cardamom or cumin.

SUPER SIMPLE YOGHURT
Serves 2

120 ml (4 fl oz/½ cup) plain yoghurt
  with active cultures (or from a
  previous batch of homemade yoghurt)
1 litre (34 fl oz/4¼ cups) non-homogenized whole milk

You will also need:
1 thermometer for liquids

Gently heat the milk to 82°C (180°F) then allow it to cool to 43°C (110°F). Stir in the yoghurt and transfer the mixture into a large glass container. Cover the container with a kitchen towel or plate and put in a warm place about 65°C (150°F), such as a heated (but turned-off) oven or the airing cupboard, overnight or wrap the container with towels. In the morning the yoghurt will have grown and thickened. Transfer to glass jars and refrigerate. When the yoghurt is cold, serve it. Keeps for 3–5 days in the fridge.

Tip: Use the kind of yoghurt and milk you prefer; sheep, cow, goat, soy, almond milk, etc.
Tip: If you prefer a thicker yoghurt, you can strain it.
Tip: You can add any flavour you like – spices, herbs or fruits – when the yoghurt has grown and thickened.

HOMEMADE NUT OR OAT MILK
Makes 750 ml (26 fl oz/3 cups)

150 g (5 oz/1 cup) raw nuts (almonds, hazelnuts or
   cashew nuts etc) or 125 g (4 oz/1 cup) whole oat groats
a pinch of sea salt
1 tsp spices of your choice (cardamom
   seeds, vanilla bean, cinnamon sticks,
   cloves, etc)

You will also need:
1 piece of cheesecloth/muslin for a fine sieve
1 large glass container

Start by soaking the nuts or whole oat grouts. Place
them in a bowl or jar, cover with twice as much water
and leave to soak for 6–8 hours or overnight.
Rinse well and place in a blender with 750 ml
(26 fl oz/3 cups) water and a pinch of salt. Blend on
high speed for about a minute. Place the cloth or
sieve over a jug and pour the blended mixture into
it. Strain the milk until only the pulp is left. Use your
hands to squeeze out the last drips of milk.
Add spices, if you wish, and place in the fridge for
about an hour. Drink it, use it in smoothies or pour
it over your porridge. The milk keeps for about three
days in an airtight container in the fridge.
To make your own nut cream, follow the instructions
for milk, but halve the amount of water.

HOMEMADE NUT & SEED BUTTER
Makes about 300 g (10½ oz/2 cups)

300 g (10½ oz/2 cups) raw nuts or seeds
   of choice
1 tsp sea salt
1 tsp grounded spice of choice (optional)

Preheat the oven to 140°C (275°F/Gas 1). Spread
the nuts on a baking tray and roast in the oven for
20 minutes, or until golden. Remove from oven and
cool slightly. If the nuts have skins, tip them off the
tray onto a clean tea towel and rub gently to remove
the skins.
Add the nuts, salt and spices (if using) to a high-speed
blender or food processor and purée for about 3–5
minutes. Depending on how powerful your machine
is, this could take even longer. Stop regularly to scrape
down the sides. Keep puréeing until the nuts turn into
a smooth and creamy paste. Scrape into an airtight
container and refrigerate. Keeps for about a month.

Tip: You can make raw nut butter by skipping the
roasting step, but it requires a high-speed blender. It
will take a little longer for the nuts to release their oils
and become a smooth butter. Add sweetener, spices,
herbs or superfood of any kind to this recipe. Add
towards the end of processing the nuts.
Tip: If you would like the butter to be creamier, add
1–2 tablespoons of neutral oil, such as cold-pressed
safflower, sunflower or grapeseed, while blending.

HOW TO MAKE FRESH SPROUTS

You can either use store-bought sprouting jars
or make your own:
1 glass jar
1 cheesecloth/muslin or clean nylon stocking
1 rubber band

Ingredients:
1 part dried beans, lentils or seeds
2–3 parts water

Soaking times:

Green lentils, red lentils, black lentils: 8 hrs

Mung beans, adzuki, chickpeas, corn: 8–12 hrs

Buckwheat, amaranth: 30 minutes

Sesame, fenugreek, broccoli, alfalfa, pumpkin
  (pepita) seeds: 8 hrs

Wheat, spelt, rye, oat, barley, kamut, millet, rice: 7–12 hrs

Yellow peas, green peas: 8–12 hrs

Sunflower seeds, quinoa: 2 hrs

Almond, hazelnut, walnut, pecan, cashew nut
(NB these nuts do not show a sprouting tail and
are therefore called 'soaks'): 4–8 hrs

Brazil, macadamia, pistachio, pine nut, hemp seeds:
do not need to soak unless your recipe requires it.

Rinse your seeds in a sieve under cold running water,
then pick out any imperfect seeds.

Transfer your seeds into the sprouting jar/s.

Add 2–3 times as much fresh water and cover with
the screen lid or cloth and rubber band. Leave to soak
(see soaking times).

Drain off the liquid. Rinse the seeds until the water
runs clear and drain very thoroughly. Set your
sprouting jars in a bright place (out of direct sunlight)
at room temperature. Rinse and drain the contents a
couple of times a day. They will be ready in 1–3 days
or when the sprouting tail is as long as the seed.

Store in sealed containers in the fridge and use within
1–2 weeks.

HOW TO COOK BEANS

250 ml (9 fl oz/1 cup) dried beans
750 ml (26 fl oz/3 cups) water for soaking, plus
  more water for cooking
½ onion
1 carrot
2 bay leaves
½ tsp sea salt

Start by removing any stones and dried-up
discoloured beans. Place the dried beans and water
in a container and leave to soak for 6–8 hours (or
overnight). Drain and rinse the beans and place in a
thick-bottomed saucepan with a lid. Add over water
until it is about 2½ cm (1 in) above the beans, then
add the onion, carrot and bay leaves.

Bring to a boil then reduce the heat and simmer,
covered, until tender. This will take approximately
45–90 minutes, depending on the variety of beans.
Add salt when the beans are just tender. They are
done to perfection when you can mash one between
two fingers or with a fork. Drain off the liquid.
Store cooked beans in the fridge where they will keep,
covered, for 4–5 days.

BASIC METHODS

RAW DATE SYRUP
Makes about 750 ml (15 fl oz/2 cups) syrup

175 g (6 oz/1 cup) medjool dates, stoned
1 tbsp lemon juice
a pinch of sea salt

Place 360 ml (12 fl oz/1⅓ cups) water, dates, lemon juice and salt in a high-speed blender or food processor. If you are using a food processor, start with a little less water and add gradually. Run until you have a smooth syrup. Use instead of honey, agave or maple syrup. Keep in an airtight container in the fridge for a couple of weeks.

APPLE SYRUP
Makes about 250 ml (9 fl oz/1 cup) syrup

1 kg (2.2 lb) apples
or
750 ml (26 fl oz/3 cups) unfiltered apple juice

Start by juicing the whole apples in a juicer. Place the apple juice in heavy-based saucepan over high heat. Bring to a boil, lower the heat to medium and simmer for 45–60 minutes, stirring occasionally.
The apple juice will cook down to about one-third of its original volume and form apple syrup. Leave to cool slightly before pouring into an airtight container. Keeps in the fridge for up to one month.

Tip: You can flavour the syrup by adding spices during cooking. Star anise, clove, cinnamon, vanilla, saffron, ginger or cardamom are all delicious with this intense and sweet apple taste.

APPLE KETCHUP
Makes about 600 ml (20 fl oz/2½ cups)

2 tbsp olive oil
2 spring onions (scallions), finely chopped
1 kg (2.2 lbs) ripe tomatoes, diced (about 10 large)
1 small red apple, diced
3 tbsp apple cider vinegar
4 tbsp raisins
1 small banana, sliced
1 tbsp tomato purée (paste)
¼ tsp sweet paprika
1 tsp whole cloves
1 cinnamon stick
3 bay leaves
sea salt
freshly ground black pepper

Heat the oil and sauté the onions on a medium-low heat in a heavy-based saucepan until soft, but not brown. Then add the rest of the ingredients and bring to a boil, lower the heat and let gently simmer for 40 minutes.
Remove the cloves, cinnamon and bay leaves. Taste and adjust the seasoning if necessary. Purée the ketchup with a hand (immersion) blender or leave it chunky if you prefer. Rise a glass jar in boiling water. Pour the ketchup into the jar while it is still warm and seal immediately. Store in the fridge for up to 2 weeks.

Mornings

One of the things we love most about our apartment is the high ceiling and large windows. They give that feeling of space that is very rare to find in an inner-city apartment. The only time we don't love our windows is in the mornings. The sun sneaks in way too early during the summer and, like a clock, I feel Elsa kicking in my ribs: 'Mor, mor vakna, jag vill spise frukost!' ('Wake up Mummy, I want breakfast!'). Obviously, we are not morning people, but if it's something – err someone – who has given us better breakfast habits, it's our daughter.

Elsa pulls us out of bed and into the kitchen right after she wakes up. And since we had her, we have actually started to eat breakfasts together. Before that, David had a coffee on his way to work and I took a smoothie with me to the gym. Now we sit there, around the breakfast table, eating together and talking. Two hours ahead of schedule.

With all that time in the morning, we now have much more varied breakfasts. We often make porridge, but some days we have fruit salad, and other days a slice of cheese on thin crispbread. We still make smoothies, but nowadays we eat them from a bowl, topped with granola. All of these breakfasts are included in this chapter, along with many more. Some of them can be whipped up in 5 minutes (like Thin Omelette Rolls, page 54), while others take 24 hours (like Dark Danish Rye Bread, page 58), so, hopefully, you will be able to find something that fits your morning habits too.

– *Luise*

Baked Crunchy Blackberry Oatmeal

400 g (14 oz/3¼ cups) fresh blackberries (thawed if using frozen)
175 g (6 oz/2 cups) rolled oats
1 tsp baking powder
½ tsp ground ginger or 1 tsp grated fresh ginger
a pinch of sea salt
2 eggs
500 ml (17 fl oz/2¼ cups) Almond Milk (see page 27) or milk of choice

1 tsp pure vanilla extract
60 ml (2 fl oz/¼ cup) Apple Syrup (see page 30) or liquid honey, maple syrup or agave
1 tbsp coconut oil (at room temperature), plus extra for greasing the pan
80 g (3 oz/¾ cup) pumpkin seeds
80 g (3 oz/generous ½ cup) hazelnuts

Serves 4–6

This is a typical Sunday morning recipe for us. We take turns on who gets to stay in bed, while the other gets up with Elsa to prepare this porridge and put it in the oven. And then we all jump back into the bed, Elsa watches a cartoon while we slumber. Half an hour later, a wonderful scent of vanilla and nuts has spread all over our apartment, and we are ready to get up. The taste and texture is actually a combination of baked oatmeal and fruit crumble.

Preheat the oven to 190°C (375°F/Gas 5). Grease the base of a 20 x 25 cm (8 x 10 in) baking dish with coconut oil and spread the berries into an even layer in the dish, then set aside.

Combine the rolled oats, baking powder, ginger and salt in a mixing bowl. In a separate bowl, beat the eggs, add the milk and vanilla and whisk well to combine.

To create the crunchy top layer, put the apple syrup, coconut oil, pumpkin seeds and hazelnuts in a small bowl and mix with your fingers to make sure everything is well coated.

Spoon the oat mixture into the baking dish to cover the blackberries, and then pour the egg mixture over the oats so everything is evenly soaked. Sprinkle the seed and nut mixture on top and bake for 35–40 minutes. When it's done, the oatmeal should be set and the nuts and seeds lightly browned and crunchy. Leave to cool slightly before serving.

Tip: For a vegan alternative: measure 2 tbsp chia seeds into a small bowl and add 90 ml (3 fl oz/¹/₃ cup) water. Stir with a spoon and place in the fridge for 15 minutes. Use in place of the eggs.

Tip: For a gluten-free alternative, choose gluten-free oats.

Herb & Asparagus Frittata

8 large eggs, whisked
250 ml (8½ fl oz/1 cup) soy milk
  or milk of choice
4 tbsp green pesto
½ tsp sea salt
2 tbsp olive oil, coconut oil
  or Ghee (see page 25)
2 spring onions (scallions),
  finely chopped
4 small potatoes (or 1 small sweet
  potato), thinly sliced
125 g (4 oz/¾ cup) cabbage,
  shredded
3 fresh asparagus spears, pared
  in ribbons with a potato peeler

Serves 4

If you peek in through our kitchen window on a random weekday morning you may well be watching us cooking an omelette or a frittata! It's part of our weekly repertoire. Our frittatas rarely look the same; we use whatever leftover vegetables we have in the fridge. This version is great when you have a few stalks of asparagus and some pesto. Shave the asparagus thinly and arrange on top of the frittata after it has baked or just towards the end of the baking time.

Preheat the oven to 200°C (400°F/Gas 6).

In a medium-size mixing bowl, whisk together the eggs, milk, half the pesto and salt. Set aside.

Heat the olive oil in a 20 cm (8 in) ovenproof frying pan on a medium heat. Add the onions, potato slices and cabbage. Stir with a spatula to make sure everything gets evenly fried. After about 5 minutes, when the vegetables are lightly golden and tender, remove to a plate and set aside. Add a little extra oil to the pan, then pour in the egg mixture. Leave for about a minute, and then scatter the vegetables evenly on top of the egg. They will sink down into the mixture, but this way they won't get burned on the bottom. Fry for a minute, while carefully loosening the edges and bottom with a spatula. Transfer the pan to the oven and cook for about 2–3 minutes, or until the frittata is golden brown on top and just cooked through in the middle. Remove from the oven, drizzle over the remaining pesto, top with asparagus ribbons and serve.

Stone Fruit Salad with Creamy Goat's Cheese

20 cherries, stoned and halved,
  plus a few whole to decorate
6 apricots, halved, stoned
  and sliced
2 saturn (flat) peaches, halved, stoned
  and sliced
2 peaches, halved, stoned
  and sliced
4 small plums, halved and stoned
1 handful of redcurrants or whitecurrants
60 ml (2 fl oz/¼ cup) Elderflower
  Lemonade (see page 203) or
  unsweetened apple juice
100 g (3½ oz/scant ½ cup) creamy goat's
  cheese

Serves 4

After a trip to Barcelona a few years ago, we came home with three large bags of fruit, vegetables and cheese from the market La Bouqueria. We worked our way through them and ended up with a bag of stone fruit and a big chunk of goat's cheese. So we turned them into a salad. It was a completely unplanned combination and it tasted so good together. You can have this dish for breakfast, but it is also nice as dessert or a lunch if you add some rocket (aragula) leaves and more vegetables.

Prepare the fruit and place in a mixing bowl. Drizzle with elderflower lemonade and toss until all the fruit is coated. Leave for 15 minutes for the fruits to release their juices. Serve on a plate and sprinkle with the crumbled goat's cheese. Decorate with a few whole cherries or fresh elderflowers, if they are in season.

Flour-Free Banana & Coconut Pancakes

3 ripe bananas
6 eggs, lightly beaten
50 g (2 oz/½ cup) desiccated
  coconut, plus extra for sprinkling
150 g (5 oz/1 cup) blueberries (fresh
  or thawed if frozen)
½ tsp ground cinnamon
2 tsp coconut oil, for frying
2 tbsp of maple syrup or plain
  yoghurt, for topping (optional)

Makes 10 pancakes

These pancakes are nothing less than a family classic. We always prepare a large stack of them when we make brunch. We have been making them for years and shared the recipe with most of our relatives and friends. And from what we have heard, they have passed the recipe on to their friends. The pancakes have a lovely fruity flavour and are easy and quick to make. What is also great is that they only call for very few ingredients, are completely flour-free and still very thick and rich. They also make a quick snack anytime of day, and a perfect post-workout meal.

Mash the bananas with a fork. Place in a medium-sized bowl and whisk together with the eggs and coconut. Add the blueberries (reserve a few for serving) and stir well.

Heat the coconut oil in a 25 cm (10 in) non-stick frying pan over a medium heat. Add two to three tablespoons of batter for each pancake. You should be able to fit 3 to 4 pancakes in at a time. Use a spatula to carefully flip the pancakes when they have set and the bottom is golden – about 2 minutes on the first side and 1 minute on the other.

Stack the pancakes and top with the reserved blueberries. On weekends we like to drizzle ours with maple syrup or yoghurt and sprinkle with a little extra coconut.

Breakfast
Blend

2 large apples, juiced, or 225 ml
  (8 fl oz/1 cup) unsweetened
  apple juice
juice of 1 lemon
1 avocado, stoned and peeled
10 brazil nuts, soaked in cold water
  for 2–6 hours
a handful of sprouted mung beans
  (see page 28), or use bought
1 cm (½ in) fresh ginger, grated
1 tbsp dried nettles
4 mint leaves
a couple of ice cubes

Serves 2

*This is a blend that we sometimes
make as an alternative to yoghurt
and top with either fruit or granola.
It is actually just like a smoothie, but
we like to serve it in bowls instead
of glasses for breakfast. Not only is it
delicious, but also very rich in proteins
and minerals thanks to the nuts and
sprouted mung beans.*

Juice the apples and lemon in a juice machine. Alternatively, use apple juice and squeeze the lemon by hand. Pour the juice into a blender and add the rest of the ingredients. Puree on high speed until smooth. Serve in bowls and top with nuts, fruits, sprouts or granola.

Tip: For extra power add wheatgrass, spirulina, hemp, protein powder, bee pollen, rosehip powder or aloe vera.

Swedish Crispbread

250 ml (8½ fl oz/1 cup) lukewarm water
2 tsp sea salt
3 tsp fast-action dried yeast
2 tbsp cumin seeds
120 ml (4 fl oz/½ cup) cultured buttermilk, filmjölk or kefir
250 g (9 oz/1²⁄₃ cup) wholegrain rye flour

225 g (8 oz/1½ cup) wholegrain spelt flour
40 g (1½ oz/¼ cup) linseed (flaxeeds), crushed (use a pestle and mortar or buy pre-crushed)
2 tbsp coarse sea salt

Makes 12 breads

You won't find a Scandinavian family that doesn't have crispbread at home. It's how we are raised. If you haven't tried it before, don't expect a bread, it's more like a cracker. When baking this, we can't emphasize enough the importance of making it thin. The thinner you make it, the crispier it becomes. It tastes fantastic with a nice cheese, thin slices of cucumber and some freshly ground black pepper. Crispbread is famous for keeping for several months when stored in an airtight container, but we usually finish a batch within a week!

Pour the lukewarm water into a medium-sized bowl. Add the salt, yeast and 1 tablespoon of the cumin seeds and stir with a wooden spoon. Stir in the buttermilk.

In a separate bowl, sift the rye flour and spelt flour together and add half of it to the yeast mixture. Gradually add more flour until the dough comes together enough for you to start kneading it. Knead for a couple of minutes in the bowl, adding more flour if it sticks to your hands. Divide the dough into 12 small buns, around 5 cm (2 in) wide and place on a floured surface. Cover with a damp cloth and leave to rest for 1 hour.

Preheat the oven to 200°C (400°F/Gas 6). Place one of the buns on a sheet of baking paper and use a rolling pin to roll it into a very thin disc, about 20 cm (8 in) diameter. Cut a small hole out of the centre of each to ensure even crispness. Sprinkle some cumin seeds, linseeds and sea salt over the dough as you roll it.

Prick each disc with a fork all over, then transfer to a baking tray. Depending on the size of your oven, you can fit one or two breads on each baking tray. Bake for around 8 minutes, until crisp and brown. Continue to roll out the rest of the buns, but always keep an eye on those in the oven. They are so thin that they go from baked to burned in no time. Cool on a wire rack.

Flowered Granola

BASIC INGREDIENTS
175 g (6 oz/2 cups) rolled oats
175 g (6 oz/2 cups) rolled rye
   or rolled spelt
150 g (5 oz/1 cup) nuts (such as
   almonds, hazelnuts or walnuts)
   roughly chopped
40 g (1½ oz/¾ cup) coconut flakes
100 g (3½ oz/scant 1 cup) seeds (such
   as sunflower and pumpkin)
1 tsp ground spices (such as
   cardamom, nutmeg, clove or
   cinnamon)

LIQUIDS FOR ROASTING
4 tbsp liquid sweetener (such as apple
   syrup, honey, agave nectar or maple
   syrup)
4 tbsp coconut oil, melted (or water)

DRIED SUPERFOOD
80 g (3 oz/½ cup) mix of dried
   nordic super berries (cranberries,
   rosehips, blackcurrants, redcurrants,
   sea-buckthorn or elderberry),
   unsweetened
4 tbsp edible dried flowers (or use
   flower blend for herb tea)

Makes about 1.5 l (3 pts/6 cups)

We prefer to keep our granola simple – a few basic ingredients, some dried fruit and a natural sweetener. We usually add more spices during the winter and fewer in the summer. Use this recipe as a base, and then add your own favourite fruit, seeds and spices. We often prepare a batch of granola to give as gifts for Christmas and moving-in parties. Just wrap it in a nice old jar or paper bag with a homemade label.

Preheat the oven to 180°C (350°F/Gas 4). Line a baking tray with parchment paper.

Combine all the basic ingredients in a large bowl. Pour the liquid ingredients over and use your hands to toss until everything is well mixed and the dry ingredients are coated. Spread the granola mixture out in the baking tray and roast in the oven for 15–20 minutes. Stir with a wooden spoon a couple of times during roasting to keep it from getting burned.

Remove from the oven and leave to cool before adding the dried superfood. Add some extra spices if needed. Store the granola in a sealed glass jar at room temperature. Keeps for at least a month.

Thin Omelette Rolls with Apple & Cottage Cheese

Serves 1

OMELETTE
- 1 egg
- 1 tbsp Almond Milk (see page 26), or milk of choice
- a pinch of sea salt
- 1 tsp Ghee (see page 25), coconut oil or olive oil for frying

FILLING
- ½ red apple, cored and coarsely grated
- 3 tbsp plain cottage cheese
- a pinch of ground cinnamon
- 1 tbsp pumpkin seeds
- a few sprigs of thyme, leaves picked, optional

Although Elsa eats almost anything we put in front of her, pancakes have always been a favourite. When we have time we make a large batch of Flour-free Banana & Coconut Pancakes (see page 45) for all of us, but when we are in a hurry we make these. It is actually a thin omelette, but Elsa calls it pancake. What is so great is that you don't have to make a whole batch. This recipe is for a single serving, but you could of course make more.

Whisk the egg, a splash of milk and a pinch of salt rapidly with a fork in a glass or small bowl. Heat the ghee or oil in a 20 cm (8 in) non-stick frying pan over a medium-high heat. Add the egg mixture and fry for 1 minute on the first side and 30–45 seconds on the other. Use a spatula to carefully flip the omelette.

Combine the filling in a small bowl. Place the omelette on a plate, spoon the filling in the middle and roll it up. Cut in half before serving. Also makes a good breakfast on the run, if wrapped in sandwich paper.

Buckwheat & Ginger Porridge

200 g (7 oz/1¼ cup) hulled whole
  buckwheat
50 g (2 oz/⅓ cup) dried fruit
  (prunes, apricots, cranberries,
  pear or whatever you have at home,
  roughly chopped if large)
1 tbsp fresh grated ginger
2-3 cinnamon sticks
1 tsp cardamom seeds
½ tsp vanilla extract
a tiny pinch of sea salt
fresh blueberries and inca berries,
  to serve

Serves 4

*Scandinavia has a long porridge
tradition. In Copenhagen they even
have a café entirely devoted to* grød
(porridge). *So it might not come as a
surprise that we love porridge in our
family. David's mum taught us this
recipe and it has become my absolute
favourite porridge. It has a fantastic
texture from the whole buckwheat;
crumbly yet soft. And it is gluten-free.
We sprinkle generous amounts of
grated ginger over it before serving,
but that is, of course, optional. Top
it with seasonal fresh fruit or the Fig,
Rhubarb & Pear Compote on
page 160.*
– Luise

Rinse the buckwheat in water, then add it to a medium saucepan
together with 600 ml (20 fl oz/2½ cups) water and the other
ingredients. Bring to a boil and lower the heat. Gently simmer
for about 20 minutes, stirring occasionally.
When the water is absorbed, the porridge should be just about ready,
but keep stirring for a few more minutes to get a crumbly texture
Remove the cinnamon sticks and serve in bowls with fresh fruit,
grated ginger and oat milk.

Tip: Rinse the cinnamon sticks in cold water and re-use them.

Dark Danish Rye Bread

190 g (6½ oz/1 cup) whole rye grains

60 g (2 oz/½ cup) sunflower seeds

500 ml (17 fl oz/2 cups) boiling water

250 ml (8½ fl oz/1 cup) plain yoghurt, at room temperature

3 tbsp clear honey

1 tbsp sea salt

1 tbsp fennel seeds

125 g (4 oz/1 cup) dried

cranberries, for flavouring (optional)

5 tbsp carob powder (or cacao powder)

4 tsp fast-action dried yeast

400 g (14 oz/2⅔ cups) whole rye flour

150 g (5 oz/1 cup) whole spelt flour

60 g (2 oz/½ cup) light spelt flour

Makes 1 loaf

We knew from the minute we started testing recipes for this book that we wanted to include Danish rye bread. Like all Danish families, we often have a dark loaf at home. We have experimented with at least 10 different ways of doing this quicker, but it always affects the quality and flavour. Baking Danish rye bread is, and will always be, a 24-hour project. But it is worth it. It is full of flavour, has a fantastic thick but moist texture, and keeps you nourished for hours. Top it with our Crunchy Curried Egg Salad (see page 176) and you have yourself a classic Danish smørrebrød.

Place the rye grains and sunflower seeds in a bowl and cover with the boiling water. Let sit for 15 minutes, then add the yoghurt, honey, sea salt, fennel seeds, cranberries and carob powder and stir with a wooden spoon. Use your finger to test the temperature of the mixture – it should be just warm.

Stir in the yeast. Then add rye flour and stir until you have a smooth batter. Cover the bowl with clingfilm and leave for 1 hour at room temperature, until the dough is slightly bubbly. Gradually add in enough of the spelt flour to form a dough. Turn out onto a floured work surface. Knead for about 5 minutes, adding the remaining spelt flour until it is firmer, but still slightly sticky and quite heavy. Form it into a ball and return to the bowl. Slap some water on the top with your hands. Cover with clingfilm and chill for 8–10 hours, or overnight.

Place the dough into a 1 kg (2¼ lb) oiled loaf tin and press down with your fists to get rid of any air pockets. The dough should be quite sticky. Brush the top with water and dust it with rye flour. Cover with a kitchen towel and set aside to rise slightly for 2 hours.

Preheat the oven to 200°C (400°F/Gas 6). Bake the loaf on the lowest shelf for 1 hour. Turn off the heat and leave the loaf in the oven for a further 15 minutes. Remove from the tin and leave to cool on an wire rack for at least 4 hours. This is important to allow the bread to set, which makes it easier to cut. Keep for about one week.

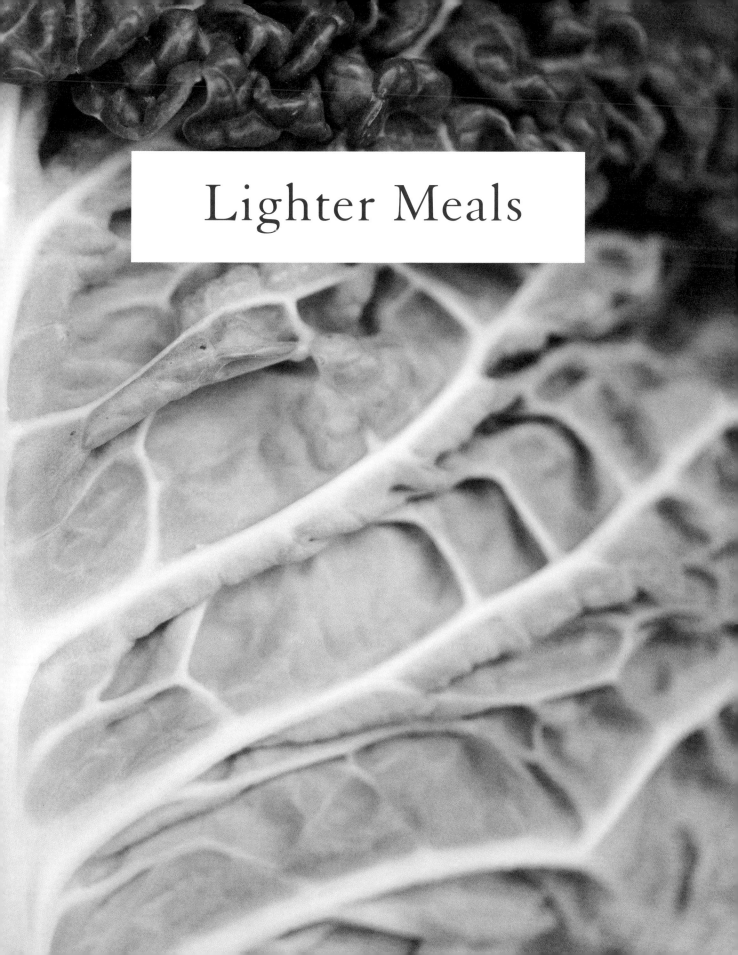

Lighter Meals

Every Friday we have a delivery of locally harvested seasonal vegetables and fruit. Although we never know exactly what awaits us in the box, we can expect fresh asparagus in April, gooseberries in July and tomatoes in August. It's our way of keeping it seasonal even though we live in a city apartment, far from crops, fruit trees and tractors. The small, shiny apples, with the blossoms and half of the branch still on, will probably be snatched in an instant. Apart from those, we usually save most of the contents until after the weekend because it is usually during the weekdays that we have most use for them.

We prefer our weekday meals to be light and if they are quick to make, we love them even more. One of the simplest and best way of using the flavourful and crispy vegetables and fruit from our box is to add them to a salad, together with a handful of toasted seeds, some sprouted lentils and perhaps also a slice of goat's cheese. That's perfect for us. It could be our Tuesday lunch as well as our Thursday dinner (but then we would probably add some Dijon and lemon marinated quinoa). Simple food that allows the ingredients to shine – this is the kind of food you will find in this chapter. Salads, a few soups, a fresh nettle pesto, a pizza crust made with cauliflower and our own version of tacos (wrapped in savoy cabbage leaves).

Baked Herb & Pistachio Falafel

FALAFELS
8 sprigs of mint, leaves picked
8 sprigs of parsley, leaves picked
240 g (8½ oz/generous 2 cups)
  pistachio nuts, shelled
400 g (12 oz/2 cups) chickpeas
  (garbanzo beans), cooked or canned
2 garlic cloves
½ small onion
3 tbsp extra virgin olive oil
1 tsp ground cumin
1 tbsp buckwheat flour (or another
  gluten-free flour)
1 tsp baking powder (baking soda)

CASHEW NUT DRESSING
6 tbsp cashew butter (or other Nut
  Butter, see page 27)
6 tbsp rapeseed oil
3 tbsp lemon juice
a pinch of salt

TOMATO CHILLI SALSA
3 tomatoes, diced
½ red chilli, seeded and finely
  chopped
1 garlic clove, finely chopped
3 tbsp olive oil
2 tsp chopped oregano
salt and freshly ground black pepper

Makes about 24 falafels

We love falafel, but we do not understand why it is always made into greasy, deep-fried fast food. Although fast food can be nice at times, we mostly prefer our meals on the lighter side. So we decided to make our own version and change some essential details. First of all, we pack it with fresh spices and pistachio nuts, which give it a wonderful colour, flavour and texture. We have never been fans of deep-frying and therefore we oven-bake our falafels. Lastly, we wrap them up in thin and crispy cabbage leaves instead of pitta bread. Try it, we promise you that you have never had a falafel that makes you feel so good afterwards.

TO SERVE
1 cabbage
240 ml (8 fl oz/1 cup) Raita
  (see page 89)
1 handful grapes, grapes halved
50 g (2 oz/1/3 cup) sunflower seeds,
  toasted
green leaves fresh herbs

FOR THE FALAFELS
Preheat the oven to 190°C (375°F/Gas 5).
Blend the herbs in a food processor for about 30 seconds. Add the pistachio nuts and pulse until well combined. Add the falafel ingredients into the food processor and blend for about a minute, stopping and scraping down the sides as necessary. Try to keep the texture of the falafel paste a little rough.
Remove the paste and, using your hands, form 24 small round falafels. Place on a baking tray covered with baking paper and bake for about 15 minutes. Turn them every 5 minutes to get an even brown colour.

FOR THE CASHEW NUT DRESSING
Whisk all the ingredients together in a small bowl until they are combined.

FOR THE TOMATO CHILLI SALSA
Put everything in a serving bowl and stir to combine. Season to taste. Refrigerate for 30 minutes to intensify the flavours.

ASSEMBLING
Turn the cabbage upside down and remove the cone with a sharp knife. Rinse it under running water and gently separate the large outer leaves one by one. Pat them dry with paper towels. Prepare all the accompaniments in small bowls and place on the table so everyone can assemble their own falafel.

Tom Kha Tofu

4 kaffir lime leaves
2 tbsp extra virgin olive oil (in Thailand they mix a bit of sweet chilli paste in the oil, to get the red colour)
1 fresh red chilli, seeded and finely chopped
16 coriander (cilantro) leaves
8 cherry tomatoes, halved
4 stalks of lemongrass
10 cm (4 in) galangal (or fresh ginger), peeled and coarsely chopped

1 litre (34 fl oz/4¼ cups) coconut milk
2 handfuls oyster mushrooms (or crimini mushrooms), halved
150 g (5 oz/2 cups) white cabbage, sliced
349 g (12 oz) block firm tofu, cut in quarters
juice of 2 limes
a pinch of sea salt
a few coriander (cilantro) leaves, to serve

Serves 4

When Elsa was 6 months old we travelled around the world together. We spent 2 months in Thailand and Tom Kha Tofu became one of our favourite meals. It is basically a mild coconut milk soup with a lime flavour, filled with mushrooms, tofu, cabbage and tomato. We got to know the chef at a lovely little restaurant, and luckily she was happy to share the recipe with us. The kha root, also known as galangal or blue ginger, is authebtic in this dish.
It's available from Asian stores or larger supermarkets, or use fresh ginger instead.

Remove the thick mid-rib from the kaffir lime leaves, roll them up tight and chop them very finely.

Put the oil, chilli, coriander and tomatoes in 4 bowls and set aside.

Crush the lemongrass and galangal, using the back of a knife, and put them in a large saucepan together with the coconut milk. Bring to a boil, then lower the heat and add chopped lime leaves, mushrooms, cabbage, tofu, lime juice and salt. Let it gently simmer on low heat for 3–4 minutes. Taste and add more salt if needed.

Pour the soup over the tomatoes and spices in the bowls, garnish with fresh coriander and serve.

Broccoli Salad with Pomegranate & Raisins

2 heads of fresh broccoli
1 small red onion, finely chopped
arils from 1 pomegranate
150 g (5 oz/1¼ cups) raisins
75 g (2½/generous ½ cup)
  sunflower seeds, toasted
250 ml (8½ fl oz/1 cup) plain yoghurt
½ tsp sea salt
freshly ground black pepper

Serves 4

This is a wonderful quick salad that has a nice crunchy texture and fresh flavours. Sweet raisins and fresh pomegranate meet raw broccoli, coated in a yoghurt dressing – you are in for a taste experience. It is great as a side dish or as a light lunch with a slice of toasted rye bread.

Separate the broccoli florets from the stalk and cut them into smaller, bite-sized pieces. Cut the remaining stalk in half and finely slice. Place in a serving bowl, together with the onion, pomegranate arils, raisins and sunflower seeds. Toss to combine. Add the yoghurt, salt, and pepper, to taste. Use your hands to mix together making sure that all broccoli florets are coated in yoghurt. Serve.

Tip: The traditional way to make this salad is with mayonnaise. Our version is lighter but you could use mayonnaise instead or use half and half.
Tip: For a vegan alternative, use soy yoghurt.

Quinoa, Cauliflower & Ramsons Cakes

200 g (7 oz/1 cup) white quinoa,
200 g (7 oz/1⅔ cups) cauliflower florets
1 large handful ramsons (wild garlic or
  ramps), coarsely chopped
4 eggs
200 g (7 oz/1⅓) feta cheese,
  crumbled
80 g (3 oz/¾ cup) rolled oats
sea salt and freshly ground black pepper
2 tbsp Ghee (see page 25), coconut oil
  or olive oil, for frying

Makes 12 cakes

*We often take whatever leftovers
we have, scrape them together with
some goat's or sheep's cheese, and fry
them into small cakes that we eat
with a salad or a coleslaw. It's often
quinoa, but sometimes also millet,
buckwheat or oats. During the spring
we always get fresh bundles of ramsons
from David's mum and that is
our favourite way to flavour these
cakes. If you cannot find ramsons,
use fresh spinach and add 2 cloves
of crushed garlic.*

Cook the quinoa – place 500 ml (17 fl oz/2¼ cups) water, the quinoa and salt in a medium-sized saucepan. Bring to a boil, lower the heat and gently simmer for about 15 minutes, or until you see small tails on the quinoa seeds. Drain any excess water and set aside to cool.

Place the cauliflower in a food processor and pulse until it is a rice-like texture. Tip into a bowl, together with the quinoa and the other ingredients. Stir with a spoon until well combined. Place in the fridge to set for 30 minutes.

Take the mixture and form into 12 patties with your hands. Heat the ghee or oil in a large frying pan on medium-high heat. Add 4 patties at a time and fry for about 3–4 minutes, or until golden brown. Flip carefully and fry the other side for 2–3 minutes more. Continue until all the patties are fried. Drain on paper towels.

Serve warm or cold; both are delicious.

Tip: For a gluten-free alternative, choose gluten-free rolled oats.

LIGHTER MEALS

Wild Nettle Pesto

150–200 g (5–7 oz) young nettle
  leaves, picked
a large handful of basil leaves, picked
1–2 garlic cloves, according to taste
juice of ½ lemon
80 ml (2½ fl oz/⅓ cup) olive oil
40 g (1½ oz/¼ cup) pine nuts,
  lightly toasted
30 g (1 oz/¼ cup) grated Pecorino

Makes about 125 g (4 oz/½ cup)

*Even though we – out of stupidity –
tried this recipe with nettles that grow
in the park just around the corner
from our apartment, we wouldn't
recommend using city nettles. We
learned afterwards that these little
stingers actually live on nitrogen,
and absorb all the bad stuff that flows
around in a city. But if you are in
the countryside during spring, pick
the tops off young nettle plants. They
are packed with iron and, as well as
making this pesto, you can also make
soup or add them to the Quinoa,
Cauliflower & Ramsons Cakes on
page 71. When crushed or mixed
they lose their sting, but don't forget
to wear gloves when picking them.
We love this pesto with wholegrain
pasta, but it also makes a great spread
for bread or a dip sauce for raw
vegetables.*

Add half of the olive oil and all of the other ingredients to a mortar,
blender or a food processor. Pound or blend, while gradually adding
the oil, until everything is combined and is a glistening paste. Taste
and add more oil, lemon, salt or pepper if required.
Bring a large pot of water to the boil. Cook the spaghetti according
to the packet instructions. Drain, return to the pan, add the pesto and
toss until coated. Serve while still hot.

Wild Rice, Artichoke & Grape Salad

10 Jerusalem artichokes
  (sunchokes)
2 tbsp extra virgin olive oil
salt and freshly ground black pepper
2 sprigs of thyme
200 g (7 oz/generous 1 cup) wild
  rice, rinsed
20 red grapes, halved and seeded,
  if necessary
150 g (5 oz/2 cups) red
  cabbage, shredded
handful of watercress (or other
  salad leaves)

DRESSING
60 ml (2 fl oz/¼ cup) extra virgin
  olive oil
juice and zest of 1 small
  organic orange
2 sprigs of thyme
salt and freshly ground black pepper

Serves 4

This is one of the prettiest salads we know. It is quite simple, but it could easily be served at a fancy dinner party when it would be a good idea to sprout the rice instead of cooking it (which makes it even prettier and more nutritious). This salad combines earthy wild rice flavours with sweetness from the roasted Jerusalem artichokes and fresh grapes.

Preheat the oven to 200°C (400°F/Gas 6).
Scrub the Jerusalem artichokes and cut them into 1 cm (½ in) slices. Place them on a baking tray, drizzle immediately with olive oil, and sprinkle sea salt and fresh thyme. Roast in the oven for about 45 minutes or until soft in the middle and golden and slightly crispy on the outside. Meanwhile, prepare the rice. Bring 750 ml (25 fl oz/3 cups) water to the boil, add the wild rice and a teaspoon of salt. Reduce the heat and let it gently simmer, covered, for 40 minutes or just until the kernels puff open. Drain off any excess water.
Whisk the dressing ingredients together in a bowl and set aside. Place artichokes and rice in a large bowl. Add the grapes, cabbage and dressing and toss lightly, using your hands, so all ingredients are coated. Garnish with sprigs of watercress and serve warm or cold.

Roasted Tomato & Chickpea Soup

1 kg (2 lb 3 oz) ripe tomatoes, halved
450 g (1 lb/2⅔ cups) cooked chickpeas
   (garbanzos)
4 sprigs of oregano, leaves picked
1 tsp paprika
6 garlic cloves, crushed with the back
   of a knife
2 tbsp extra virgin olive oil
sea salt
plain yoghurt and a few oregano leaves,
   to garnish

Serves 2–4

We often keep the most beautiful tomatoes on our kitchen counter, but forget to use them. They sit there waiting patiently. You can almost see how they start jumping for joy every time our hands come close. Days pass, and they turn riper and riper until one day they are almost too ripe to use. That is when we bake and mix them into this soup. It has a wonderful roasted, mild flavour and a creamy texture thanks to the chickpeas. You can, of course, use fresh young tomatoes instead, but we have found that very ripe tomatoes have a more intense, sweet flavour.

Preheat the oven to 200°C (400°F/Gas 6).

Place the tomatoes, chickpeas, oregano, paprika and garlic on a baking tray. Drizzle with olive oil, place in the oven and bake for about an hour, or until the tomatoes are slightly blackened in places and bubbling. Remove from the oven (save a few chickpeas for serving) scrape all ingredients into a blender or food processor and blend until smooth.

Add a little water if needed. Serve in bowls or glasses, with a dollop of yoghurt, fresh oregano leaves and a few roasted chickpeas on top. Delicious served with a slice of sourdough bread.

Savoy Tacos with Corn & Mango Filling

Serves 4

If we had to choose one dish that defines our way of cooking, this version of tacos would probably be a good suggestion. They combine vegetables with fruit and beans, they are served in leaves rather than bread, and they look spectacularly beautiful. Did we mention that they also are filled with a detonation of flavours?!

CORN AND MANGO FILLING
2 corn cobs
450 g (1 lb/2⅔ cups) cooked black beans, drained (see tip)
1 small spring onion (scallion), finely chopped
1 mango, peeled and sliced
30 g (1oz/½cup) dried coconut flakes
grated zest and juice of 1 lime
1 tbsp extra virgin olive oil
1 tsp ground cumin
1 pinch each of cayenne, paprika, and dried oregano
sea salt

RAW SOUR CREAM SAUCE
150 g (5 oz/1 cup) raw cashew nuts, soaked in cold water for at least 1 hour
1 tbsp apple cider vinegar
juice of ½ lemon
a pinch of sea salt

TO SERVE
1 savoy cabbage or spring (collard) greens
2 ripe avocados, stoned, peeled and sliced
1 large handful of coriander (cilantro), leaves picked and chopped

FOR THE TACO FILLING
Use a sharp knife to cut off the corn kernels from all sides of the cobs and place them in a mixing bowl. Add the beans, spring onion, mango, coconut flakes, lime zest and juice, olive oil and spices. Toss gently with your hands to make sure that everything is coated. Set aside.

FOR THE RAW SOUR CREAM SAUCE
Add all the ingredients to a blender and purée until completely smooth. If you like it a bit runnier add some water. Pour the sauce into a bowl and put in the fridge while you prepare the cabbage.

ASSEMBLING
Turn the cabbage upside down and remove the cone by cutting around it with a sharp knife. Rinse it under running water and gently separate the leaves one by one. Pat them dry with kitchen paper. Remove the middle rib with a sharp knife and cut each leaf in two.
Place the leaves on a work surface, put a spoonful of filling onto each leaf, followed by a little raw sour cream sauce and a few avocado slices. Top with coriander before folding over the cabbage leaf and securing with a toothpick. Alternatively, place all the taco components on the table and let people help themselves.

Tip: if you prefer this dish raw, use sprouted beluga lentils instead of cooked black beans in the filling.

LIGHTER MEALS

Lemony Fennel & Lentil Salad

FOR THE MARINADE
juice of 1 large lemon
2 tbsp clear honey
sea salt
freshly ground black pepper

FOR THE SALAD
1 fennel bulb and leaves (they look like dill), sliced paper-thin
4 large handfuls of crisp lettuce
1 cucumber, peeled, seeded and sliced
200 g (7 oz/1 cup) green lentils, sprouted (see page 28) or cooked
200 g (7 oz) creamy ash-coated goat's cheese roll, cut into 1 cm (½ in) slices

Serves 4

I think both David and I were served too much lettuce when we were kids. For a long time we rarely felt like making anything with it, even if we had a whole head in our fridge. Most of the time, it just went straight to the compost. I know now what a waste that was. Fresh crispy lettuce has both character and a nice texture; it just needs to be paired well. This is the salad that helped us appreciate it again. Crisp lettuce is topped with thin slices of lemon-marinated fennel, protein-rich green lentils, locally grown cucumber and thick slices of ashed goat's cheese. Eat as it is or serve as a side dish for a barbeque gathering.
– Luise

Whisk the marinade ingredients together in a small bowl. Place the slices of fennel in a shallow dish then pour the marinade over. Toss with your hands so that all slices are coated. Set aside for 10 minutes. Put the lettuce in a large bowl, add the cucumber and lentils, then add the marinated fennel together with the juices and toss around. Tuck in slices of goat's cheese and serve.

Pizza with a Cauliflower Base

florets from 1 cauliflower
80 g (3 oz/¾ cup) ground
  almonds
1 tbsp dried oregano
sea salt and freshly ground black
  pepper
3 eggs, beaten

Makes 1 pizza

This recipe is for a healthier pizza crust. Cauliflower instead of flour – crazy right?! It is, in fact, super-tasty and really quick to make. No leavening needed, just mix it up and bake. You can find several topping suggestions on pages 142–43, or use any of your own favourites.

Preheat the oven to 200°C (400°F/Gas 6) and line a baking tray with baking paper.

Coarsely chop the cauliflower, place in food processor and blend until it is a fine rice-like texture. Measure 600 ml (20 fl oz/3 cups) of the cauliflower 'rice' and place in a mixing bowl. Add the ground almonds, oregano and seasoning and mix with your hands. Make a well in the centre and add the eggs. Use your hands to pull the dry ingredients towards the middle until everything is combined and you can shape it into a ball. It should be more loose and sticky than traditional pizza dough.

Transfer to the baking paper and form into a pizza base by flattening the dough with your hands. Make the edges slightly higher. Bake for about 25–30 minutes, or until golden.

Meanwhile, prepare a pizza topping of your choice. Remove the pizza from the oven. Cover it with topping and put it back in the oven for about 5–10 more minutes.

Tip: For a vegan alternative, replace the eggs with this chia mixture: measure 30 g (1 oz/¼ cup) of chia seeds into a bowl and add 175 ml (6 fl oz/¾ cup) of water. Stir well and place in the fridge for 15 minutes before use.

Indian Chickpea Crêpes with Raita & Leafy Greens

Makes 12 cakes

RAITA
- 225 ml (8 fl oz/1 cup) plain yoghurt
- 1 cucumber, peeled, seeded and shredded
- 4 large sprigs of mint, leaves picked and very finely chopped
- 2½ cm (1 in) fresh green chilli, seeded and very finely chopped
- 1 garlic clove, crushed
- 1 tsp cumin seeds

CHICKPEA CREPES
- 250 g (9 oz/2 cups) chickpea (garbanzo) flour
- ½ tsp ground turmeric
- ½ tsp ground cayenne
- ½ tsp ground ginger
- ½ tsp curry powder
- ½ tsp ground coriander
- ½ tsp kalonji seeds
- 1 tsp sea salt
- 600 ml (20 fl oz/2½ cup) carbonated (soda) water
- Ghee (see page 25) or coconut oil, for frying
- 200 g (7 oz) leafy greens, to serve

Soft in the middle with crispy edges, these are the perfect crêpes – and yet they are made without any egg or milk. The secret ingredients are carbonated water and protein-rich chickpea (garbanzo) flour, called besan flour which you can find in Asian markets or health food stores. We have spiced them up with a host of Indian flavours.

Start by preparing the raita. Place all the ingredients in a medium-sized bowl, stir together and put in the fridge for 30 minutes before serving. In a large bowl, sift together the chickpea flour, spices and salt. Whisk in the soda water and put the batter in the fridge for 30 minutes. When you are ready to start cooking, heat the oil in a large, non-stick frying pan on a medium heat. Pour around 75 ml (2½ fl oz/⅓ cup) batter into the pan and give it a good swirl so that it spreads thinly across the entire pan. Wait until the base of the pancake is a deep golden colour, then flip with a spatula and cook the other side until golden and cooked through. Repeat until you have used up all the batter.

Serve the crêpes warm with leafy greens and raita. Also delicious served alongside a stew, such as the Rhubarb, Apple & Yellow Split Pea Stew on page 116.

Tip: For a vegan alternative, use soy yoghurt.

Good to Go

On sunny days we often pack some leftovers and a blanket in a basket and walk to a park just down from where we live. Stockholm is nice that way. There are parks, water and green areas in every part of the city. So even though we don't have a terrace, balcony or garden, we get to eat outside pretty often during the summer months.

We also go on more planned picnics. Elsa gets all giddy whenever we visit the city farm, which is only a bus ride away. We usually take some wraps or muffins to eat and she gives an apple to the horses. And we sometimes take a small ferry to Rosendals Trädgård, a lovely garden where you can eat a picnic under the blossoming apple trees in spring. When Elsa was three months old, we arranged a picnic there so all our relatives and friends could come and meet her. Everybody brought food, which we shared together under a large oak tree.

In this chapter we have listed some recipes that can survive a few hours in a picnic basket without looking sad. For example, our picnic bread roll, with vegetables hidden inside, a delicious cold potato salad and small fennel and coconut tarts. All these dishes would also be great to take to a gathering during the winter.

Savoury Corn & Millet Muffins

130 g (4½ oz/⅔ cup) raw millet
125 g (4 oz/1 cup) cornmeal
125 g (4 oz/1 cup) rice flour
2 tsp baking powder (baking soda)
1 tsp bicarbonate of soda
1 tsp sea salt
3 eggs, beaten
225 ml (8 fl oz/1 cup) soya yoghurt, or yoghurt of choice

120 ml (4 fl oz/½ cup) extra virgin olive oil
around 25 (3 tbsp) kalamata olives, stoned and halved
200 g (7 oz/ 1⅓ cups) crumbled feta cheese
3 sprigs of oregano, leaves picked

Makes 12 medium-sized muffins

Baking gluten-free bread can be a challenge for anyone, as it often requires special ingredients and many different flours. Gluten-free muffins, however, are a lot easier. We often bake a vegan version of these as a midday snack for Elsa's preschool. We use olives, but any savoury filling will work just as well.

Preheat the oven to 180°C (350°F/Gas 4). Line a muffin tin with muffin cases.

Cover the millet with 120 ml (4 fl oz/½ cup) boiling water and let sit for 5 minutes, then rinse in cold water. This is to extract the bitter taste from the millet shell and to make it softer. Mix the millet with the cornmeal, rice flour, baking powder, bicarbonate of soda and salt.

In another bowl, beat the eggs until fluffy. Add the yoghurt and olive oil and stir together. Add to the dry ingredients and stir with a wooden spoon until everything is incorporated. Add the olives, feta cheese and oregano and stir well.

Spoon about two heaped spoonfuls into each muffin case. Bake for about 20 minutes, rotating the tin halfway through to make sure the muffins are evenly cooked. They are ready when golden and crusty on top. Best served warm.

Tip: For a vegan alternative, omit the feta cheese and replace the eggs with chia seeds. Measure 3 tbsp chia seeds in a bowl and add 100 ml (3½ fl oz/scant 1 cup) water. Stir well and place in the fridge for 15 minutes before using.

Fennel & Coconut Tart

TART CASE
- 65 g (2¼ oz/ generous ½ cup) rice flour
- 45 g (1¾ oz/scant ⅓ cup) almond flour (or chestnut flour)
- 2 tbsp potato flour, tapioca flour or cornflour (cornstarch)
- ½ tsp sea salt
- 3 tbsp coconut oil or Ghee (see page 25)
- 3 tbsp ice-cold water

FENNEL FILLING
- 120 ml (4 fl oz/½ cup) coconut milk
- 2 eggs, beaten
- ½ tsp grated nutmeg
- 2 sprigs of rosemary, leaves picked and chopped
- sea salt and freshly ground pepper
- 1 fennel bulb, very thinly sliced

Makes 1 large 20 cm (8 in) tart or 4 small 10 cm (4 in) tarts

Fennel is a beautiful vegetable and we have often talked about how we can let it shine properly. Our Lemony Fennel & Lentil Salad on page 84 is one attempt, but I think this tart is an even better example. The sweet coconut filling enhances its characteristic anise-like flavour. No cheese is needed here! The gluten-free case is made with almond flour and has sweet flavour and just the right consistency.
– David

To make the tart case, sift together the flours, starch and salt in a bowl. Add the coconut oil and ice-cold water and use your hands to work the dry ingredients towards the centre until a dough forms. If it feels crumbly, add 1–2 tablespoons more water. Gather it into a ball, wrap in clingfilm and chill for 30 minutes in the fridge.

Meanwhile, make the filling. Whisk the coconut milk, eggs, nutmeg, rosemary, salt and pepper together in a small bowl until combined. Preheat oven to 190°C (375°F/Gas 5).

Use your hands to press the dough evenly into the bottom and up the sides of the tart tin. If making four smaller tarts, divide the dough into four equal pieces before pressing into the tins. Trim the dough flush with edge of the tin and prick the base with a fork to prevent the pastry from rising as it bakes.

Pour the coconut and egg mixture into the tart case then place the fennel slices on top. Place in the middle of the oven and bake for about 35 minutes or until the tart is golden and crispy.

Tip: Make the dough a day ahead. Wrap tightly in clingfilm and leave in the fridge until you're ready to use it.

GOOD TO GO

Beetroot, Apple & Goat's Cheese Wraps

Makes 8 wraps

PURPLE BEETROOT FILLING
375 g (13 oz) raw beetroot (red beets)
  (about 4–5 medium-sized)
300 g (10½ oz/1¼ cup) soft
  goat's cheese
sea salt and freshly ground pepper

ORANGE QUINOA FILLING
200 g (7 oz/1 cup) white quinoa,
  rinsed
1 tsp fennel seeds
a pinch of sea salt
finely grated zest and juice of
  ½ orange
75 g (2½ oz/generous ½ cup) raisins
100 g (3½ oz/scant 1 cup) toasted
  walnuts, chopped
8 wholegrain or corn tortillas or large
  spring (collard) green leaves
4 large spinach leaves (torn in two)
2 avocados, stoned, peeled and sliced
3 small eating apples, grated

No food is more appropriate to take on a picnic than wraps. They keep very well, you don't need cutlery, and they can be made in endless varieties. We usually like to combine a few different fillings in our wraps to make them more interesting to eat. Raw beetroot is a favorite of ours. It tastes much fresher than cooked, especially when combined with apple and goat's cheese. Raisins are added for sweetness and walnuts for crunch. Lentils would also be a great addition.

To prepare the beetroot filling, peel the beetroot, cut into quarters and place in a blender or food processor, then pulse a few times to finely chop. Add the goat's cheese and salt and pepper. Blend for about 30 seconds or until the mixture has the consistency of a rough-textured spread. Taste and add more salt or pepper if needed. If you don't have a blender or food processor, use a grater to shred the beetroot and use your hands to mix the grated beets and the crumbled goat's cheese together.

For the quinoa filling bring 500 ml (17 fl oz/2¼ cups) of water to a boil in a small pan. Add the quinoa, fennel seeds and salt and gently simmer for about 15–20 minutes, until tender and the liquid is absorbed. Set aside too cool. When cold, add the orange zest and juice, raisins and walnuts and stir to combine.

ASSEMBLING

Put 2–3 spoonfuls of the beetroot filling in the middle of each tortilla (not all the way to the edge) and cover with half a spinach leaf. Place a couple of spoonfuls of the quinoa filling on top and finish with some slices of avocado and grated apple.

Fold the top and bottom edges over the filling. Roll the whole tortilla from left to right to wrap in the filling. Roll some baking paper around them and tie with string to hold them together while you transport them. Done! Cut the wraps in half before serving.

GOOD TO GO

Apple & Mushroom-stuffed Picnic Bread Roll

1 tbsp fast-action dried yeast
250 ml (8½ fl oz/1 cup) water,
  heated to about 40°C (100°F)
1 tbsp clear honey
1 tbsp sea salt
200 g (7 oz/1¾ cup) light spelt flour
225 g (8 oz/1½ cup) whole spelt
  flour
2 tbsp extra virgin olive oil

FOR THE FILLING
  3 tbsp extra virgin olive oil
  ½ leek, sliced
  1 garlic clove, minced
  10 crimini (or button) mushrooms,
    quartered
  1 green eating apple, peeled, cored
    and cut into 1 cm (½ in) pieces
  juice of ½ lemon
  60 g (2 oz/½ cup) grated Pecorino
  3 sprigs thyme, leaves picked
  freshly ground black pepper

Makes about 10 portions

I first tried this brilliant bread while living in Italy. They typically make it for Easter, but I'd say it's even more perfect for summer picnics. Instead of putting a topping on top of baked bread, it is hidden inside the bread before baking and as you break off the first piece, you unveil what's inside. This is our suggestion for a delicious savoury filling, but you could make it into a dessert by adding extra sweetness to the dough and filling it with fruit, honey and mascarpone cheese.

Put the yeast in a large bowl, add water, honey and salt and stir until dissolved. In a separate bowl, sift the flours together, and then add half to the yeast mixture. Stir with a wooden spoon before gradually adding the rest of the flour. Knead in the bowl for a minute, then knead on a floured surface for a few minutes more. Add more flour if it feels too sticky. You want the dough to be elastic but not sticking to your hands. Rub the olive oil over the dough and form it into a ball. Return it to the bowl, cover with clingfilm and leave to rise for about 1 hour.

Meanwhile, prepare the vegetable filling. Pour 1 tbsp olive oil in a frying pan on a medium heat. Add the leek and garlic and sauté for a few minutes. Add the mushrooms and apple and fry for 3–4 minutes, stirring regularly. Season with salt and pepper. Remove from the heat, squeeze over the lemon juice and leave to cool.

When the dough has risen, re-knead briefly on a floured surface. Place the dough on a sheet of baking paper. Roll out a rectangle, around 30 x 40 cm (12 x 16 in) and around 1 cm (½ in) deep. Drizzle with the remaining olive oil. Spread the filling evenly on bottom half of the dough and sprinkle with the Pecorino. Top with the thyme and some pepper. Use the baking paper to roll the dough into a log. Brush one of the ends with water then form the dough into a ring. Pinch the two ends together to form a closed tube. Place on a baking tray. Sprinkle with flour and leave to rise under a tea towel (dish cloth) for 30 minutes.

Preheat the oven to 200°C (400°F). When the roll has risen, bake for about 35–40 minutes, or until golden. Good warm or cold.

GOOD TO GO

Potato Salad with Dill & Horseradish

1 kg (2 lb 3 oz) small new potatoes
15–20 small heirloom tomatoes, halved
200 g (7 oz/2 cups) fresh sugarsnap
  peas, sliced lengthwise
1 large handful of dill, coarsely
  chopped

DRESSING
  2.5 cm (1 in) fresh horseradish, grated
  2–3 tbsp apple cider vinegar
  2–3 tbsp extra virgin olive oil
  sea salt and freshly ground pepper

Serves 4

Not only is this salad beautiful, with the multi-coloured heirloom tomatoes, sugarsnap peas, potatoes and dill scattered all over, it is also packed with flavour and acidity from freshly grated horseradish and apple cider vinegar. It's one of our favourite summer salads. We often have this as a side dish at barbeque parties.

Place the potatoes in a saucepan with just enough cold salted water to cover. Bring to a boil then reduce to simmer for 15 minutes. Test with a small sharp knife – when the potatoes fall off the knife they are done. Drain and set aside to cool.

Meanwhile prepare the tomatoes, sugar peas and dill and place in a large serving bowl. Whisk together the dressing ingredients in a small bowl. When the potatoes are cold place them in the serving bowl, pour the dressing over and toss with your hands so everything is coated. Serve.

Maple-tossed Beluga Lentil Salad

200 g (7 oz/1 cup) beluga or
  puy lentils
2 thin, red rhubarb sticks,
  thinly sliced
20 strawberries, sliced
150 g (5 oz/scant 1 cup) shelled
  edamame beans
small handful of fresh redcurrants,
  optional
8 asparagus spears, chopped into
  2.5 cm (1 in) pieces
15 basil leaves

DRESSING
  3 tbsp maple syrup
  3 tbsp extra virgin olive oil
  juice of ½ lemon
  sea salt and freshly ground
    black pepper

Serves 4

This salad is a celebration of all the wonderful fruit and vegetables that are in season during the spring. Raw rhubarb is sliced thinly and tossed in a maple dressing, which gives both tartness and sweetness. Beluga lentils are great in picnic salads as they stay firm even after a bumpy car ride.

Rinse the lentils under running water. Transfer to a medium saucepan, together with 500 ml (17 fl oz/2¼ cups) water and bring to a boil. Reduce the heat and gently simmer for about 15–20 minutes or until tender. When almost done, add a pinch of salt, then drain and set aside to cool.

Prepare all the salad ingredients and place in a large bowl, together with the cooled lentils. Whisk together the ingredients for the dressing, add to the salad and toss with your hands until everything is well coated. Top with a couple of basil leaves.

Divide between four small glass jars, cover with lids and you are ready to go. Serve with a piece of sourdough bread.

Tip: This is a vegan recipe, but you could crumble 100 g (3½ oz) feta cheese and place a quarter in each jar to make it even more nourishing.

Strawberry Gazpacho

600 g (1 lb 5 oz/4 cups) fresh
   strawberries, hulled and halved
500 g (1 lb 2 oz) watermelon,
   seeded and cut into 2.5 cm (1 in)
   chunks
1 red (bell) pepper, seeded
   and chopped
2 small spring onions (scallions),
   halved
15 mint leaves
juice of ½ lemon
1 celery stick, chopped
4 drops of Tabasco (or more
   to taste)

Serves 4–6

*We love the concept of a chilled soup
and although we appreciate a classic
gazpacho, we often prefer to make this
slightly sweeter version. Instead of
tangy tomatoes, this soup oozes fruit.
We balance it with onion, celery, mint
and a few drops of Tabasco.*

Put all the ingredients in a blender or a food processor. Pulse until you
have a soup consistency, taste it and add more salt, pepper or lemon
if needed. Store in a large bottle in the fridge. If you are taking it to a
picnic, put a few ice cubes in the bottle just before you leave so it stays
cool. Take along a few glasses for serving.

GOOD TO GO

Family Dinners

In our living room we have a very beautiful, big dinner table. I got it from my mother, and I think she got it from her father. It's a wooden table, probably more than 100 years old, with scratches and marks from dinners in the past. We really love that table. Unfortunately I have a hunch that it doesn't love us back because we never eat on it. Sometimes we come there with a bowl full of food, only to take a photo for the blog. Or we use it to sort papers or put Elsa's toys on. I realise how insulting it must be for a table with that kind of history, but it is just how things have turned out. As much as I love that table, it is just easier eating in the kitchen, close to all our pots, pans, pepper and salt.

The only time we do use our dinner table is when we have friends or family over for a meal. Then we fill it with plates, cutlery and glasses (we never use a cloth, scratching the table has always been part of the deal). We dim the lights in our living room and put on a Nina Simone record. When, later during the night, I listen to the buzz as everyone is talking and eating, glasses clinking and chairs scraping the floor, I always think 'we should do this more often'. And probably, so does our table.

The dinners in this chapter should be nourishing enough to satisfy both vegetarians and meat-eaters. Although unintentional, we have managed to squeeze in recipes inspired from Sweden, Morocco, Italy, France, India and Japan. So, regardless of whether it is a birthday party for your sister, your son's school class, or your best friends coming over, we hope that you will find something to put on your dinner table.
– *David*

Sweet Apricot & Cauliflower Dal

HOMEMADE SPICE BLEND
- ½ tbsp coriander seeds
- ½ tsp mustard seeds
- ½ tsp cardamom seeds
- ½ tbsp curry powder
- ½ tsp ground cloves
- ½ tsp ground ginger
- a pinch of chilli powder
- 6 unsulphured dried apricots, chopped
- 2–3 tbsp Ghee (page 25), coconut oil or extra virgin olive oil for frying

- 1 small onion, finely chopped
- 2 garlic cloves, crushed
- 1 cauliflower, cut into florets
- 2 carrots, sliced
- 200 g (7 oz/scant 1 cup) red lentils, rinsed
- 750 ml (25 fl oz/3 cups) coconut milk
- 200 g (7 oz) spinach, coarsely chopped
- sea salt
- 1 large handful coriander (cilantro)

Serves 4

I have had a food crush on India for as long as I can remember. I have been there a few times, and am always struck by the huge variety of vegetarian food, based on lentils, beans, potatoes, cauliflower, okra, peas, paneer cheese, fruit and spices. They always manage to combine strong and bold flavours with mild and sweet, into amazing soups, stews and stir-fries. In this recipe all the different spices trigger an explosion of flavours, which is rounded off with sweet, dried apricots and coconut milk. We often make our own spice blend, which basically is a way for us to increase the flavours of the standard supermarket curry spices.
– David

Start by making the spice blend. Grind the first three spices in a pestle and mortar. Add the rest of the spices and apricots and use your fingers to mix it together.

Heat the ghee in a large saucepan on medium heat. Add the spice blend and stir constantly with a wooden spoon. Fry until it smells fragrant and looks browned, but be careful the spices do not burn. If it feels too dry add a spoonful, or more, of water.

Add the onion and garlic and fry a couple of minutes while stirring.

Add the cauliflower and carrots and stir until they are fully coated by the spices. Now add the lentils, coconut milk, and 225 ml (8 fl oz/1 cup) water and stir well and simmer, covered, for 15–20 minutes or until the vegetables and lentils are cooked through.

Add the spinach and stir through. Top with the coriander and serve as it is or with cooked brown or wild rice. Add salt to taste.

Rhubarb, Apple & Yellow Split Pea Stew

Serves 4–6

2 tbsp Ghee (see page 25), use coconut oil or extra virgin olive oil if you are vegan
1 tbsp cumin seeds, ground
½ tbsp cardamom seeds, ground
a pinch of cayenne
1 large onions, diced
4 garlic cloves, crushed
5 cm (2 in) piece of fresh ginger, finely chopped or grated
800 g (1 lb 12 oz) butternut squash, summer pumpkin or sweet potato peeled, seeded and cut into 2 cm (1 in) cubes

5 sticks rhubarb (250 g/9 oz), sliced
1 red eating apple, cored and diced
150 g (5 oz/⅔ cup) yellow split peas or yellow lentils, rinsed
sea salt
2–3 tbsp clear honey, use maple syrup if you are vegan
a handful of flat leaf parsley, to garnish, optional

Rhubarb is something most people eat for dessert, but its sweet and tangy qualities make it just as usable in savoury dishes. We learned this from our friend and brilliant cook, Sarah Britton, from My New Roots. *This recipe is inspired by hers and I think she was inspired by something Mark Bittman wrote in* How to Cook Everything Vegetarian, *so it's really third-hand here. We always keep a few boxes of rhubarb in our freezer, so we have been able to make slightly varied versions of this dish all year round. This dish is good as it is, but you can also serve it with cooked brown, black, red or wild rice.*

Heat the ghee or oil in a heavy-based pan. Add all the spices and stir constantly with a wooden spoon. Fry until they smell fragrant and look browned – be careful not to let them burn. If it looks too dry, add a spoonful water, or more. Add the onion, garlic and ginger and fry for a couple of minutes while stirring.

Add the butternut squash, rhubarb and apple and stir around to coat with the spices. Next add the split peas and 900 ml (30 fl oz/4 cups) water and simmer, covered, for 20–25 minutes, or until the vegetables and split peas are soft. Season with salt and add the honey. Serve with a good handful of chopped parsley, if using.

Portobello & Peach Burgers

6 portobello mushrooms
6 peaches
6 wholegrain burger buns
100 g (3½ oz) fresh pea sprouts
5 small tomatoes, sliced
5 small spring onions (scallions),
    sliced
a small handful of thyme leaves,
    picked

MARINADE

60 ml (2 fl oz/¼ cup) extra virgin
    olive oil
2 sprigs of rosemary (chop 1 of them
    finely and use the other as a brush)

1 tbsp of thyme, leaves picked and
    finely chopped
2 garlic cloves, finely chopped
juice of ½ lemon
sea salt and freshly ground black pepper

GUACAMOLE

4 ripe avocados, halved, stoned and
    peeled
3 small tomatoes
1 handful flat-leaved parsley
1 clove garlic
½ lemon
2 tbsp extra virgin olive oil

Makes 8 wraps

Although over the years we have made several different versions of veggie and bean burgers, patties and cakes, nothing is quite like a grilled portobello mushroom burger. It is the simplest, most natural and delicious piece of food you can put inside a burger bun. It is big, chewy and actually strikingly burger-looking, and when heated it releases moisture and becomes all flavourful and juicy.

We like to top our burgers with mashed avocado, fresh tomatoes, sprouts and some kind of fruity salsa. Here we have replaced the salsa with peaches that are grilled with the mushrooms. Serve with our Spicy Skinny Root Sticks (see page 178) and some homemade Apple Ketchup (see page 30).

Clean the portobello mushrooms by carefully removing dirt from the caps with kitchen paper or a cloth; use a little water if necessary. Cut off the stems and discard. Pat dry. Cut the peaches in half and remove the stones.

Make the guacamole – chop the avocados, tomatoes and parsley roughly. Put them in a small bowl with the crushed garlic, squeeze lemon juice over and mash everything with a fork. It should be mixed but still a bit chunky. Set aside.

Now make the marinade – pour the olive oil into a small bowl. Add the chopped rosemary, thyme, garlic, freshly squeezed lemon juice and stir to combine. Add salt and pepper to taste. Use the other rosemary sprig to brush the mushrooms and peaches with the marinade.

Preheat a griddle pan and griddle the mushrooms and peaches for about 3–4 minutes on each side over high heat. Alternatively, you can barbeque them. Use the rosemary sprig to brush the marinade over them as they cook.

Slice the buns in half and toast them lightly on the grill. When done, place a big dollop of guacamole on the bottom bun, add pea sprouts, tomatoes, spring onion, thyme, one mushroom and two peach halves. Add the top of the bun, and insert a cocktail stick to hold it all together.

Beet Bourguignon

2 tbsp extra virgin olive oil
1 brown onion, chopped
4 garlic cloves, finely chopped
8 small beetroots (red beets), peeled and quartered (we used Chioggia beets)
6 carrots, sliced in large pieces
3 bay leaves
2 sprigs of thyme
sea salt and freshly ground pepper
2 tbsp tomato purée (paste)
250 ml (8½ fl oz/1 cup) red wine, use vegan wine if you are vegan

500 ml (17 fl oz/2¼ cups) vegetable stock
400 g (14 oz/2 cups) puy lentils
a pinch of sea salt
2 tbsp extra virgin olive oil
2–3 portobello mushrooms, sliced
10 crimini mushrooms
10 pearl onions, peeled
2 tsp arrowroot, dissolved in 2 tbsp water
a few springs of thyme, leaves picked, to garnish

Serves 4

Most people are familiar with Julia Child's classic recipe for Bœf Bourguignon. Talk about making an impression and leaving a footprint. Her Bœf Bourguignon is made with beef and bacon, so not the most appropriate dish for vegetarians, but we reckoned that there must be a way to transform that rich, wine-oozing hot pot into something more to our taste. After a few experiments it turns out that we were only one letter away. We turned beef into beet. We also added large chunks of mushrooms to give the stew the right texture and flavour. Our Root Mash (see page 149) is also a good companion.

Heat the olive oil in a thick-bottomed saucepan or Dutch oven over a medium heat. Stir in the onions and garlic and sauté until soft. Toss the beetroot, carrots, bay leaves, thyme and salt and pepper into the pan and cook for 5 minutes, stirring occasionally.

Stir in the tomato purée, red wine and vegetable stock and simmer on low heat for 20 minutes.

Meanwhile, rinse the lentils under running water. Bring 1 litre (2 pts/ 4 cups) of water and the lentils to a boil. Lower the heat to medium and simmer gently for 15–20 minutes. When almost cooked, add the salt. Drain off any excess water, cover and set aside.

Now heat the olive oil in a large frying pan, lower the heat and sear the mushrooms and pearl onions, stirring occasionally, until tender and golden in colour. Season to taste and set aside.

Taste the stew and add more wine, stock or herbs if you like. Add the arrowroot mixture. Stir gently, just until thickened and clear. Add the mushrooms and onions and simmer for 10 more minutes. Remove the bay leaves and thyme sprigs before serving. Spoon the stew into 4 bowls together with the lentils, and sprinkle with fresh thyme.

FAMILY DINNERS

Moroccan Vegetable Tagine

3 tbsp extra virgin olive oil
1 large onion, roughly chopped
3 garlic cloves, crushed
1.5 cm (1 in) fresh ginger, grated
  (or 1 tsp ground)
1–2 tbsp ground cinnamon
1 tsp ground cumin
sea salt
2–3 tsp harissa paste (or dried harissa)
2 x 400 g (14 oz) cans whole plum
  tomatoes
grated zest and juice of 1 lemon
a large of handful coriander (cilantro),
leaves picked and chopped
1 small butternut squash, cut into 5 cm
  (2 in) pieces
1 sweet potato, cut into 5 cm (2 in) pieces
3 carrots, cut into 5 cm (2 in) pieces

1 courgette (zucchini), cut into 5 cm
  (2 in) pieces
10 unsulphured dried apricots
250 g (8 oz/1⅓ cup) chickpeas
  (garbanzo beans), cooked or canned
  and rinsed
75 g (2½ oz/½ cup) handful golden
  raisins

TO SERVE

200 g (7 oz/1 cup) wholegrain
  couscous
2 tbsp olive oil
1 l (32 fl oz/4 cups) water
roasted almonds
a small handful of fresh coriander
  (cilantro), leaves chopped
a few sprigs of fresh mint

Serves 4

*Sweet cinnamon is combined with
soft vegetables, sweet raisins and hot
spices. The trick is to get the vegetables
as tender as possible and the easiest
way to do that is by letting them slowly
steam in their own juices on a low heat
for as long as possible. A traditional
tagine is ideal for cooking this recipe,
but even with a clay pot or casserole
dish, it shouldn't be too difficult. Serve
with wholegrain couscous, quinoa or
cooked millet.*

Heat the olive oil in a large heavy-bottomed saucepan, or flameproof
casserole dish and sauté the onion for a few minutes until it softens.
Add the garlic and ginger and the spices and stir around before adding
the harissa, tomatoes, lemon juice and fresh coriander. Bring the sauce
to a boil and then lower the heat.

Add the squash, sweet potato, carrots, courgette and apricots. Stir well
so everything is covered in tomato sauce. Put the lid on and simmer
for about an hour. Keep covered, but stir carefully once or twice while
cooking. After an hour and when the vegetables are very tender, stir in
the chickpeas and raisins and cook for 5 minutes more.

If you are using a tagine, you might need to soak it before use. Preheat the
oven to 150°C (300°F/Gas 2) and prepare the tomato sauce according to
the instructions above. Set aside. Add the vegetables to the tagine, pour
over the tomato sauce, making sure all vegetables are covered, attach the
lid and put in the oven and cook for about 1½ hours. When the vegetables
feel tender, add the chickpeas and raisins and let everything cool for
5 minutes more before removing from the oven.

When the vegetables are almost ready, place the couscous in a large bowl.
Drizzle the olive oil over and stir around until coated. Pour boiling water
over the couscous and cover the bowl with a lid for 10 minutes to allow
the couscous to absorb the water. Fluff up the couscous with a fork. Serve
immediately, sprinkled with roasted almonds, coriander and mint.

Hazelnut, Aubergine & Mushroom Parcels

175 g (6 oz/1½ cups) hazelnuts, coarsely chopped
75 g (2½ oz/scant ¾ cup) raisins
1 aubergine (eggplant)
16 crimini mushrooms
4 sprigs of oregano, leaves picked

200 g (7 oz/scant 1 cup) ricotta cheese
juice of ½ lemon
1 tbsp sea salt
freshly ground black pepper

Makes 8 parcels, enough for 4 people as a main course

During the summer we often wrap vegetables and fresh herbs in foil and add to the barbeque. The intensity of the flavours that ooze out as we open them always comes as a surprise. Unfortunately the barbeque season is quite short in Sweden, so off-season we bake these parcels in our oven. We fill them with aubergines, mushrooms, ricotta and hazelnuts, and flavour them with oregano and sweet raisins. They are great at dinner parties as they require little effort. We often serve them with a polenta, but a green salad or the Potato Salad on page 105 would be good for a lighter meal.

Preheat the oven to 200°C (400°F/Gas 6). Put the hazelnuts and raisins in a large mixing bowl. Slice the aubergine into 1 cm (½ in) squares and quarter the mushrooms. Add to the bowl.

Chop the oregano coarsely and add to the bowl, together with the ricotta cheese. Add the lemon juice, salt and pepper. Stir carefully with a wooden spoon until everything is incorporated.

Cut four 25 cm (10 in) squares of baking paper. Divide the filling between the centres of the baking paper squares. Gather the corners together and tie the parcels with string. Place on a baking sheet and bake for 25 minutes.

Serve the parcels whole so that your guests can untie their own.

Hash Pan with Broad Beans

1 tbsp extra virgin olive oil
1 brown onion, coarsely chopped
2 garlic cloves, coarsely chopped
450 g (1lb) small summer potatoes,
  cut into 1 cm (½ in) cubes
3 beetroots (red beets), cut into
  1 cm (½ inch) cubes
3 carrots, cut into 1 cm (½ inch) cubes
2 parsnips, cut into 1 cm (½ inch) cubes
1 celeriac (celery root), cut into
  1 cm (½ inch) cubes
15 fresh broad (fava) beans, shelled and
  podded

1 courgette (zucchini), cut into 2.5 cm
  (1 in) cubes
a large handful of fresh dill

DRESSING
  1 tbsp mustard
  2 tbsps extra virgin olive oil
  1 tbsp clear honey or agave
  1 tbsp lemon juice

SERVE WITH
  4 egg yolks (optional)

Serves 4

*Both Luise and I loved this dish
as children. It's called* Biksemad
in Denmark and Pytt i Panna *in
Sweden, but is made in exactly the
same way – by chopping up whatever
leftovers you have and frying them
in a pan. Normally it is quite
meat-heavy, with heaps of ham and
sausages. Ours is more root-based.
We use small summer potatoes,
beetroots, parsnip and celeriac. Since
some of the ingredients have different
cooking times, the idea is to chop and
throw in the pan as you go, starting
with the potatoes and ending with
the courgettes.
– David*

Heat the olive oil in your largest frying pan on medium heat. Add the
onion and garlic and sauté for about a minute. Add the potatoes and
beetroot and fry for about 7 minutes before adding the carrots, parsnips
and celeriac. Stir occasionally to make sure the roots don't stick to the
pan. Add a little more olive oil if needed Fry for 5 minutes then add the
broad beans, courgette and a few sprigs of dill. Fry for 5 more minutes,
or until all the vegetables are tender.

Make the dressing by shaking together the ingredients in a small screw-
topped jar. Add the dressing to the pan if you like it creamy, otherwise
just have it on the side. Traditionally, it's served with an egg yolk on the
top. Incorporate it on your plate while the dish still is warm.

Tip: You can use whatever you have in your fridge in this dish.
We sometimes add spring onions, chickpeas, tofu, broccoli or
sugarsnap peas.

Courgette Noodles with Marinated Mushrooms

MARINATED MUSHROOMS
4 small Portobello mushrooms, sliced
60 ml (2 fl oz/¼ cup) extra virgin olive oil
60 ml (2 fl oz/¼ cup) apple cider vinegar

CASHEW AND TOMATO DRESSING
150 g (5 oz/1 cup) raw cashew nuts, soaked in cold water for 4–6 hours
grated zest and juice of 1 organic lemon

1 garlic clove, chopped
2 tbsp extra virgin olive oil
200 g (7 oz/generous 1 cup) marinated sundried tomatoes, drained
sea salt and freshly ground pepper

COURGETTE NOODLES
2 green or yellow courgettes (zucchini)

Serves 4

You might have heard of courgette (zucchini) noodles or maybe even tried them? They are thinly sliced courgettes eaten raw instead of regular spaghetti. This is my favourite way to dress them up. The cashew and sundried tomato dressing is full of flavour and the marinated mushrooms add tanginess and a satisfying chewiness.
– Luise

Place the sliced mushrooms in a bowl. Whisk the oil and vinegar together and pour over the mushrooms. Turn them a couple of times so they are fully coated in marinade. Cover and leave in the fridge for about an hour, stirring the mushrooms occasionally.

Add all the dressing ingredients to a blender and mix until smooth. If you do not have a blender, grind everything in a large pestle and mortar until creamy. If it feels too thick, add some water. Season to taste with salt and pepper.

Wash the courgettes and cut them lengthwise, using a julienne or mandolin slicer, so you get thin spaghetti-looking strips. Put them in a large mixing bowl. Add the dressing and mix gently, so everything is coated. Then add the marinated mushrooms and serve!

Tip: If you don't have a julienne slicer, spiralizer or mandolin slicer, you can use a potato peeler and it will come out as tagliatelle instead.

Tip: You can slice the courgette noodles and leave them to dry for about 30 minutes before storing in an airtight container in the fridge for up to 5 days.

Sushi Explosion with Wasabi Yoghurt

MARINATED TOFU
75 ml (2½ fl oz/⅓ cup) sesame oil
75 ml (2½ fl oz/⅓ cup) soy sauce
2 tbsp rice vinegar
1 garlic clove, crushed
½ red chilli, seeded and finely
  chopped
2.5 cm (1 in) fresh ginger, peeled
  and grated
300 g (10½ oz) firm tofu, drained,
  dried and cubed

BROWN SESAME RICE
400 g (14 oz/2 cups) brown, red,
  wholegrain or wild rice
a pinch of sea salt
2 tbsp rice vinegar
1 tbsp sesame oil
1 tsp chopped coriander (cilantro)

PICKLED GINGER
a large chunk of fresh ginger, approx
  12 cm (5 in), peeled and thinly siced

sea salt
60 ml (2 fl oz/¼ cup) apple cider vinegar
1 tbsp clear honey
a pinch of sea salt

WASABI YOGHURT
120 ml (4 fl oz/½ cup) plain yoghurt
1 tbsp green wasabi paste

SALAD INGREDIENTS
1 large broccoli, cut into florets
1 spring onion (scallions), thinly sliced
2 avocado, stoned, peeled and cubed
12 crimini mushrooms, cut in quarters
1 handful sugarsnap peas, halved
  lengthwise
1 small handful bean sprouts
½ cucumber, cut into sticks
8 sheets nori seaweed, cut into
  5 x 5 cm (2 × 2 in) cubes
1 tiny handful sesame seeds,
1 large handful coriander (cilantro),
  leaves picked

Serves 4

This is what happened one day when we felt like making our own vegetarian sushi, but were too lazy to go through the whole Japanese rice and roll procedure. Instead we marinated tofu, boiled some brown rice, chopped our favourite vegetables, cut the seaweed into pieces and made it look like the sushi had exploded into a bowl. We love this salad. The sesame oil, rice vinegar and seaweed give the salad that sushi feeling, but with a more nourishing twist.

MARINATING THE TOFU
Drain the tofu and pat dry with kitchen towel. Cut into 2.5 cm (1 in) cubes. Mix the ingredients for the marinade in a bowl and add the tofu. Mix until well coated. Chill for at least 25 minutes (longer if you have the time).

PREPARING THE RICE
Rinse the rice in water until it comes clear, drain and add to a saucepan with 1 litre (1¾ pints/4¼ cups) boiling water and the salt. Bring to the boil. Reduce to a simmer for 45 minutes or until tender and the water has been absorbed. Cool slightly and stir in the rice vinegar, sesame oil and coriander.

PREPARING THE PICKLED GINGER
Peel the ginger root and slice it very thinly lengthwise, place on a plate, sprinkle with salt and set aside for 15–30 minutes. Squeeze the ginger with your hands, rinse it under running water and squeeze again. Place in a small bowl.

Whisk the ingredients for the marinade together with 2 tbsp water
and pour over the ginger slices. Pickle for 15–30 minutes.

PREPARING THE WASABI YOGHURT
Stir the yoghurt and half of the wasabi paste together. Taste and add
more wasabi if you like – the flavour of the wasabi is quite different
depending on the brand you use.

ASSEMBLING
Blanch the broccoli – place the florets in a bowl and pour boiled
water over, let sit for 2 minutes, then drain and rinse in ice cold water.
Combine all the vegetables and nori together in a bowl.
Divide the rice into 4 large bowls and top with the vegetables and the
marinated tofu. Drizzle the rest of the tofu marinade over the salad and
top it with sesame seeds and coriander. Serve with the marinated ginger,
wasabi yoghurt and some soy sauce.

135   FAMILY DINNERS

Sicilian Parmigiana Di Zucchine

1 batch Basic Tomato Sauce, add
   a handful mint together with
   the basil (see page 22)
5 courgettes (zucchini)
5 eggs, hard-boiled
2 tbsp olive oil

300 g (10½ oz) buffalo mozzarella,
   drained and sliced
100 g (3½ oz/1 cup) grated parmesan
1 large handful basil, leaves picked
1 large handful mint, leaves picked
sea salt and freshly ground black pepper

Serves 4–6

This is a classic Italian recipe, similar to lasagne but layered with courgette slices instead of sheets of pasta. It is therefore a bit lighter and yet very nourishing. We use a Sicilian-inspired tomato sauce with lots of fresh mint added to it. It gives a wonderful and unexpected flavour combination.
We took a shot of the dish (opposite) before adding the final tomato sauce and parmesan top layer, so you can see how the layers should look.

Preheat the oven to 200°C (400°F/Gas 6). Thinly slice the courgettes lengthwise, about 7 mm (⅓ in) thick. Place in a large colander, sprinkle with 5 tsp of salt and toss well. Set aside to drain for 30 minutes. Meanwhile, crack and peel the eggs and cut into 7 mm (⅓ in) slices. Rinse the courgette slices and pat dry on paper towels. Preheat the grill. Brush the slices with olive oil and grill for 10 minutes or until golden, turning over after 5 minutes. You can also use a griddle pan to do this. To assemble the dish, ladle a little tomato sauce into a 25 x 30 cm (10 x 12 in) baking dish. Cover with a layer of courgettes, then mozzarella slices, egg slices, parmesan, basil leaves, mint leaves and pepper. Then repeat. You want to finish with a layer of courgette and then cover completely with the last of the tomato sauce and the parmesan.
Bake in the oven for 40 minutes or until the cheese is golden and bubbling. Remove from the oven and let it set for about 15 minutes before serving.

Red Lentil Polpette with Lemon Balm Sauce

200 g (7 oz/1 cup) red lentils
½ red onion, finely chopped
2 garlic cloves, minced
3 tbsp extra virgin olive oil
2 tbsp tomato purée (paste)
40 g (1½ oz/ ⅓ cup) rolled oats
1 tsp paprika
a pinch of cayenne, or more to taste
sea salt

LEMON BALM AND BASIL SAUCE
a handful lemon balm, leaves picked
1 handful basil, leaves picked
60 ml (2 fl oz/¼ cup) oil of choice
juice of ½ lemon
a small handful hazelnuts, toasted and skinned
sea salt and freshly ground black pepper

Makes 15 balls

One day I came home from work and Luise had prepared these vegan polpette, served with courgette noodles. It was her own version of the spaghetti and meatballs from Lady and the Tramp. *I adore her for things like that. Although I have been a vegetarian for more than half my life, I have never done anything even slightly similar. And she just threw it together on a regular Tuesday. Such an innovative take on an old classic. The lentils add a nice, sweet flavour and texture to the polpette, and go really well with the lemon balm and basil sauce. Serve with Courgette Noodles (see page 131), or with regular wholegrain spaghetti.*
– David

To prepare the polpette, rinse the lentils and place in a saucepan with 500 ml (17 fl oz/2¼ cups) cold water. Bring to the boil, lower the heat and simmer gently for 15 minutes or until tender. Drain well and cool slightly.

Mash the lentils with a fork or use an immersion/hand blender. The consistency you want is mashed but still with some whole lentils left. Place in a mixing bowl, add the remaining polpette ingredients and stir with a spoon until everything is combined. Place in the fridge for 30 minutes.

Preheat the oven to 190°C (375°F/Gas 5) and line a baking tray with non-stick baking paper. Form 15 balls with your hands, place them on the baking paper and bake for 15–20 minutes. Turn every 5 minutes to get a nice even colour and shape.

Meanwhile, make the lemon balm and basil sauce. Place all the ingredients in a blender with 2 tablespoons of water and mix until creamy. If you prefer the sauce a little runnier, add some water.

Tip: If you can't get hold of lemon balm, use more basil and add the juice of a lemon.

Tip: For a gluten-free alternative, use gluten-free oats.

Four Vegetarian Pizzas

BASIC SPELT PIZZA DOUGH

250 ml (8½ fl oz/1 cup)
  lukewarm water
2 tsp fast-action dried yeast
2 tsp sea salt
300 g (10½ oz/2½ cups) light spelt
  flour
2 tbsp olive oil

Makes 12 mini pizzas or 2 large

You know when you do something that you think you are pretty good at and then you see someone else doing it a hundred times better? That is how we felt when we ordered a vegetarian pizza from a small ristorante on Sicily, a few years back. Mama mia, it was a taste sensation! And they had thrown at least 15 different vegetables on a small pizza slice. Ever since our visit, we have been working on improving our own pizza recipes. Here we have made a few favourite combinations into mini pizzas. The amounts for the toppings are enough to make 2 large or 12 small pizzas, so just divide it if you want to make more than one kind. If you want a lighter, gluten-free pizza crust, try our cauliflower 'dough' on page 86.

Pour the lukewarm water in a medium size bowl. Add the salt and yeast and stir around. Mix in 225 g (8 oz/2 cups) of the flour. Gradually add the rest of the flour until the dough forms a ball. Knead a floured work surface for a couple of minutes, adding more flour if it sticks to your hands. Put the dough back in the bowl and rub with olive oil. Rub the dough until it's completely covered in the oil. Cover the bowl with clingfilm and leave in a warm place for 1–2 hours to prove.
Preheat the oven to the highest possible temperature 240°C (475°F/ Gas 9). Knead the dough with your hands on a lightly floured work surface. Divide it into 10 to 12 small portions. Stretch and flatten the dough until you get the desired size and thickness that you prefer and place on baking trays lined with baking paper. Spelt flour doesn't stretch as easily as wheat flour but if you work carefully and flatten it with the palm of your hand you will get it right. Another trick is to roll them out directly on the baking paper with a lightly floured rolling pin and then just move the baking paper to the baking tray.
Add the topping of your choice, bake for about 10–15 minutes until golden around the edges.

Red Sicilian Topping

½ batch Basic Tomato Sauce
(see page 22)
6 small potatoes, halved and boiled
12 slices of griddled and marinated
aubergine (eggplant) (buy ready-made
or use recipe on page 149)

12 cherry tomatoes, halved
12 mushrooms, halved
a handful of pickled capers, drained
6 small spring onions (scallions),
divided lengthwise
2 sprigs of oregano, leaves picked

Smear about two tablespoons tomato sauce on each pizza dough. Place the potatoes, aubergine, cherry tomatoes, mushrooms and capers on top. Add the spring onions and oregano and bake for about 10-15 minute until golden round the edges. You can also just use the tomato sauce, cherry tomatoes and oregano to make a simple and pretty cherry tomato pizza.

Sweet Apricot Topping

250 g (9 oz/1 cup) ricotta cheese
12 fresh apricots, stoned
and sliced
150 g (5 oz/1½ cups) fresh raspberries
120 ml (4 fl oz/½ cup) Raw Date Syrup
(see page 30)

Smear about two tablespoons of ricotta on each pizza dough. Brush the apricot slices with date syrup and arrange them in circular shape on top. Toss on a few raspberries, then bake as above.

Green Courgette Topping

200 g (7 oz/4 cups) baby spinach
120 ml (4 fl oz/½ cup) olive oil
2 garlic cloves
salt and freshly ground black pepper

12 small courgettes (zucchini), sliced
100 g (3½ oz/scant ½ cup) soft goat's cheese

This pizza has a green sauce that can be prepared in a whizz, no cooking needed. Combine the spinach, olive oil, 60 ml (2 fl oz/¼ cup) water, the garlic, salt and pepper in a blender, and purée until smooth. Smear the spinach sauce evenly over the pizza dough. Arrange the courgette slices on top of the sauce, sprinkle with crumbled goat's cheese and bake (as opposite).

White Potato Topping

1 tbsp extra virgin olive oil
12 uncooked potatoes, skin on, sliced
2 small spring onions (scallions), thinly sliced

6 sprigs oregano or rosemary, leaves picked
100 g (3½ oz) goat's cheese

Brush the dough with a thin layer of olive oil. Cover it with potato slices, onion, oregano, the goat's cheese, salt and freshly grounded black pepper. Drizzle a bit of olive oil over the pizza and bake for about 10-15 minutes until the outer part of the topping and the edges are slightly burnt.

Mascarpone Beanotto with Oyster Mushrooms & Spinach

2 tbsp extra virgin olive oil
1 large onion, finely chopped
2 garlic cloves, finely chopped
100 g (3½ oz/1½ cup) sliced oyster
  mushrooms (or button), sliced
120 ml (4 fl oz/½ cup) dry white wine
250 g (9 oz) spinach, coarsely
  chopped

450 g (1 lb oz/2⅔ cups) cooked white
  cannellini beans (see page 28)
120 ml (4 fl oz/½ cup) vegetable stock
60 g (2 oz/¼ cup) mascarpone cheese
grated zest and juice of ½ organic lemon
handful of thyme, leaves picked
sea salt and freshly ground pepper

Serves 4

Risotto has always been a hit in our family, especially during the autumn and winter months. But sometimes we prefer to cook completely grain-free dishes, and then these creamy beans hit the spot. We call it 'beanotto' because the wine flavours and the creamy consistency are very similar to a risotto. If you have pre-boiled or canned beans, this dish will be ready in 10 minutes.

Heat the olive oil in a large saucepan over a medium heat. Add the onion and garlic. Sauté for a few minutes, stirring occasionally, until softened and golden.

Add the mushrooms and fry for about a minute. Stir in the wine and spinach and simmer until the spinach has cooked down.

Now add the beans and stock. Cook and stir for 3–4 minutes. Lower the heat and add the mascarpone cheese, lemon juice and thyme. Stir well, then taste and season with salt and pepper. Serve sprinkled with grated lemon zest.

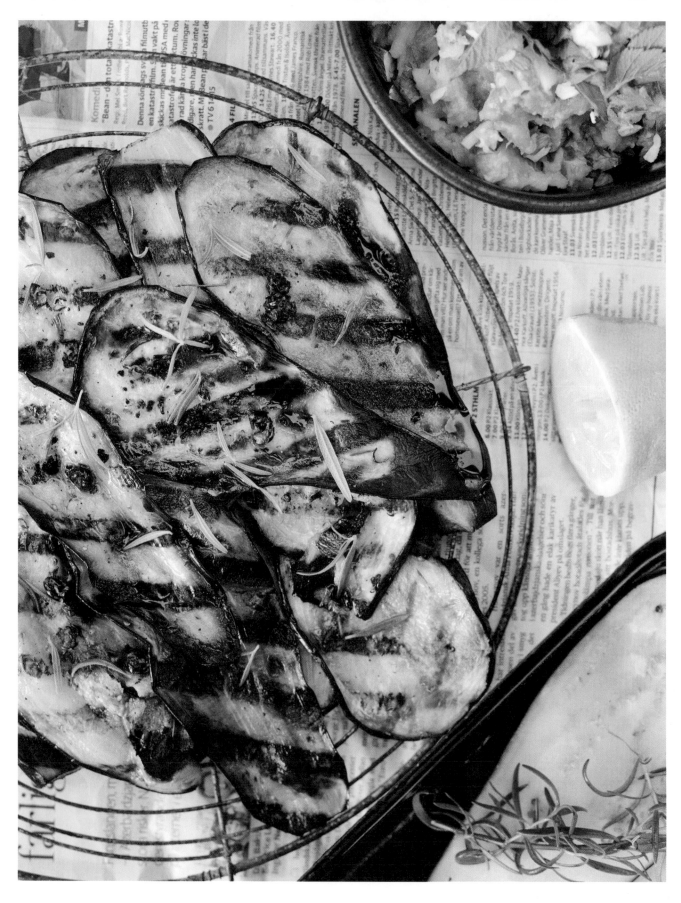

Juniper-Marinated Aubergine & Root Mash

ROOT MASH
1 kg (2 lbs 3 oz) mix of sweet potato,
   parsnip and turnip
75 ml (2½ fl oz/⅓ cup) olive oil
grated zest and juice of 1 lemon
a handful of coriander (cilantro)
   or flat-leaf parsley
100 g (3½ oz/scant ½ cup) coarsely
   chopped almonds or pecans
sea salt and freshly ground
   black pepper

JUNIPER MARINADE
1 tbsp dried juniper berries, crushed
2–3 sprigs rosemary, leaves picked
120 ml (4 fl oz/½ cup) extra virgin
   olive oil
juice of 1 lemon
sea salt and freshly ground
   black pepper
3–4 aubergine (eggplants), cut
   lengthwise into slices about
   1 cm (½ in) thick

Serves 4

The root season in Sweden is endless. They are one of the few vegetables that can actually handle this climate. We often pound them into a lemon and almond-flavoured root mash. You can make it using a food processor, but it's even better mashed by hand, with a little bit of texture left. During the summer we serve it with juniper-marinated aubergines, chargrilled just a tad too long for depth of flavour.

Rinse and peel the roots, and cut into smaller pieces. Place in a large saucepan, cover with cold water and bring to the boil. Lower the heat and gently simmer for about 15–20 minutes or until tender, it will depend on the size of your vegetables. If a knife goes through easily then they are cooked.

Remove from heat, reserve a little of the cooking water and drain off the rest. Add the oil, lemon zest and juice, coriander, nuts and seasoning and use a potato masher to mash the roots well. Use a wooden spoon to beat further, adding a splash of cooking water to achieve the consistency you desire.

Meanwhile, mix the crushed juniper berries and rosemary leaves with the oil and lemon juice to make the marinade. Season with salt and pepper. Lay the aubergine slices on a large plate or tray and cover with the marinade. Leave for 30 minutes to 1 hour to really soak up the flavours.

Preheat your grill, barbeque or griddle pan to really hot. Grill the marinated aubergines on each side, turning every minute or so. Use a rosemary sprig to brush them with more marinade. They are ready when they are soft in the middle with crispy sides and charred in stripes. Serve with the root mash and a green salad.

You will also need:
5 pieces of cheesecloth or muslin
20 x 30 cm (8 x 12 in) 10 x 5-cm
(2-in) lengths of kitchen string

Quinoa & Vegetable Chorizo Salad

VEGETABLE CHORIZOS
100 g (3½ oz/scant ½ cup) sundried
   tomatoes, rinsed
125 g (4 oz/¾ cup) cashew nuts, toasted
½ red onion, coarsely chopped
½ red chilli, seeded and finely chopped
6 unsulphured dried apricots, coarsely
   chopped
2 sprigs of oregano, leaves
   picked and chopped
200 g (7 oz/1 cup) rice flour
1 tbsp xanthan gum
1 tbsp linseed (flaxseeds), ground
60 ml (2 fl oz/¼ cup) extra virgin olive oil
1 litre (59 fl oz/4¼ cups) vegetable stock
1 tbsp olive oil, for frying

QUINOA SALAD
200 g (7 oz/1 cup) black quinoa
15 heirloom tomatoes, halved
2 small red apples, diced
½ onion, sliced
350 g (12 oz/2 cups) cooked butter
   (lima) beans (see page 28)

DRESSING
75 ml (2½ fl oz/⅓ cup) olive oil
zest and juice of ½ organic lemon
3 tbsp hot English mustard
sea salt
a few sprigs of oregano, to garnish

Serves 4

A word of warning: this recipe uses words that might freak out some vegetarians. But fear not – our chorizos are purely plant-based! This is without doubt the most unexpected dish in this cookbook. Not only have we made sausages(!) but we also threw them in a quinoa salad. It's definitely not our usual combination, but it is really good. The mustard dressing in the salad matches the chorizos perfectly. You can of course also make the quinoa salad without the chorizos (or buy ready-made). And equally, there are many ways you can eat and serve the vegetable chorizos – as a classic hot dog, in bangers and mash, or in a stew.

To prepare the chorizos, combine the sundried tomatoes, cashew nuts, onion, chilli and apricots in a food processor or blender. Pulse until finely chopped. Add the herbs, rice flour, xanthan gum and linseeds and pulse until everything is combined. Add the olive oil and 60 ml (2 fl oz/¼ cup) water and pulse until a dough is formed. It should be easy to handle and form into a sausage shape.

Divide the dough into 5 equal parts. Roll each piece into a sausage, place on the cheese cloth, roll up and tie the twine firmly around both ends. Repeat with the rest of the sausages.

Bring the vegetable stock to the boil in the widest frying pan you have. Lay the chorizos in it and let them boil for about 45 minutes. Next, carefully remove the cloths from the boiled chorizos. Heat the olive oil in a frying pan on a medium-high heat and fry them until they are nicely browned all over.

Next prepare the quinoa salad. Place 500 ml (17 fl oz/2¼ cups) water, the quinoa and salt in a heavy-based saucepan. Bring to the boil, lower the heat and gently simmer for 15–20 minutes. Drain any excess water and set aside to cool. Prepare the tomatoes, apples and onion, and slice the fried chorizos.

Whisk together the dressing ingredients in a small bowl. Put the quinoa, tomatoes, apples, onions and butter beans into a large bowl. Add the chorizo slices then pour over the dressing and toss about to make sure all the ingredients are well coated. Garnish with oregano and serve.

Amaranth & Halloumi-Stuffed Tomatoes

STUFFED TOMATOES

200 g (7 oz/1 cup) amaranth
a pinch of sea salt
50 g (2 oz/½ cup) coarsley chopped
  raw shelled pistachio nuts
100 g (3½ oz) halloumi cheese,
  coarsely chopped
3 tbsp pickled capers, drained
1 egg
6–8 large tomatoes

ROASTED ROOTS

1 kg (2lb 3 oz) roots, such as sweet
  potato, parsnip and carrots
200 g (7 oz/generous 1 cup)
  black olives
3 sprigs of rosemary
2 tbsp extra virgin olive oil
2 tsp sea salt
1 lemon, cut into quarters
1 garlic bulb, halved horizontally

Serves 4

We love efficient cooking. In this recipe the roots are roasted in the same pan as the stuffed tomatoes. Everything is ready at the same time, which always makes things easier, and the filling can be prepared a day in advance and stored in the fridge. Amaranth is a tiny, protein-packed seed that makes this dish lighter than the traditionally used rice. If you can't find amaranth use quinoa or millet instead. If you can't find halloumi cheese, use a goat's feta cheese instead.

Place the amaranth in a saucepan with 600 ml (20 fl oz/2½ cups) water cups water and salt. Bring to the boil, lower the heat to a bare simmer, cover and cook gently for 20 minutes.

Meanwhile prepare the rest of the ingredients and place them in a medium-sized mixing bowl. Drain the cooked amaranth and cool slightly before adding to the other ingredients. Stir to combine and set aside.

Use a sharp knife to cut off a cap from the top of each tomato. Carefully lift it off and remove the seeds and pulp from inside using a teaspoon. Fill the tomato shells with the amaranth mixture and pop the caps back on.

Preheat the oven to 200°C (400°F/Gas 6).

Rinse the roots. (If using organic, there is no need to peel them.) Cut into equal large pieces, around 5 x 1 cm (2 x ½ in). Place them in a large mixing bowl, together with the olives, rosemary and oil. Toss, using your hands, so all vegetables are covered with oil. Place on a baking tray, together with the stuffed tomatoes, garlic and lemon quarters, and put in the oven. Roast for 50–60 minutes, or until golden with crispy edges. Serve immediately.

FAMILY DINNERS

Small Bites

Every once in a while, we do an 'Extreme Fridge Makeover'. We empty it, clean it and David rearranges the shelves so that we, 'for the first time', will have complete order in there. The air is filled with excitement as he explains the new strategy: 'Okey Lul, listen now, vegetables go here, leftovers on the top shelf. And all your jars have their own shelf right here.' He is good at planning stuff like that. And I can really see it works, in theory. The problem is that we are no good at following those instructions and in the midst of cleaning up after dinner, if I see an empty shelf, I go for it. And so does David, no matter what he claims. So six months later, we have to start all over again.

My jars, are definitely also part of the problem – the spreads, compotes, pâtés, nut butters, fermented cabbage and homemade sweeteners that tend to multiply all over the shelves. I imagine that a good solution would be to get an extra fridge, just for all our jars. The thing is, we don't eat like traditional families. Many of our meals are accompanied by a side or a spread of some sort. Raw vegetable sticks, a bowl of goat's cheese dip, some beans on the side or a jar of baba ganoush. It's often all those bits and pieces that add up to a whole and satisfying meal.

We have collected a few of our favourite 'jars' here. But also a recipe for grain-free seed crackers, an unexpected ceviche and a plate of courgette and ricotta rolls. All of these small bites are not only good as side dishes, but would also be perfect on a buffet table.
– *Luise*

Baba Ganoush

2 aubergines (eggplants) –
   approx 800 g (1 lb 12 oz)
2 tbsp sesame oil
3 tbsp lemon juice
2 garlic cloves garlic, crushed
1 tsp sea salt
2 tbsp olive oil
1 bunch of flat-leaf parsley or coriander
   (cilantro) leaves

Makes enough to fill 1 x 350 g (12 oz) jar

Middle Eastern cuisine has so many great vegetarian spreads. Hummus is, of course, the most popular and well-known. But we'd like to highlight another favourite of ours: the baba ganoush. Its slightly tangy and smoked flavours go particularly well with pitta chips and other salt crackers. Most recipes call for sesame paste, but since it has a tendency to overpower all other flavours, we use the milder sesame oil instead.

Preheat the oven to 240°C (475°F/Gas 9).

Cut the aubergines in halves lengthwise. Place cut sides down on a baking tray lined with baking paper and roast for about 45 minutes, until completely soft with black skin. They will look punctured when they're done.

Remove from the oven and leave to cool for a few minutes. Remove the skin. It should come away easily, but if not, put them in a plastic bag for 10 minutes and then try again.

Finely chop the pulp and scrape into a medium-sized bowl. Add the sesame oil, lemon juice, garlic and salt. Stir and mash everything with a fork until smooth. Taste and add more salt and lemon juice if necessary. Chill for about 1 hour before serving. Store in an airtight glass jar in the fridge. Keeps for 3–4 days.

Smashed Peas with Almonds & Chilli

500 g (2 oz/3½ cups) shelled fresh
   peas, or frozen (thawed)
50 g (2 oz/½ cup) coarsely chopped
   almonds
juice of ½ a lemon
1–2 tsp seeded and finely chopped
   fresh chilli
1 small bunch of mint, leaves
   picked (reserve a few for serving)
60 ml (2 fl oz/¼ cup) extra virgin olive oil
sea salt

Serves 4

For some reason, we don't use peas very often. It's strange considering their sweet flavour and pretty colour. We were reminded of this when we visited a garden cafe on the island of Gotland in southern Sweden. They had a pea mash that tasted so good smeared on a slice of sourdough. As soon as we returned home, we went to the market, bought a big bag of fresh peas and made this dish. Use it as a side dish or smear it on sourdough or on Dark Danish Rye Bread (see page 158).

Place all the ingredients in a mixing bowl. Use a hand/immersion blender to purée the peas, but keep some whole to create a rough-textured mash. Taste and adjust the seasoning. Top with a few mint leaves and serve. The colour of the peas darkens rather quickly, so best eaten on the day its made.

Fig, Rhubarb & Pear Compote

150 g (5 oz) rhubarb (about 3 sticks), chopped in 2.5 cm (1 in) pieces
2 pears, peeled, cored and coarsely chopped
6 soft dried figs, coarsely chopped
2.5 cm (1 in) pieces of fresh ginger, grated
1 tbsp cardamom seeds, ground

Makes about 350 g (12 oz/1¼ cups)

Even though we don't use sugar in this compote, it is very sweet and super-delicious. The flavours are far more complex than a traditional strawberry compote, and it therefore goes really well with a cheese and seed crackers or crispbread.

Place the fruit, ginger, cardamom and 1 tablespoon water in a medium-sized saucepan. Slowly bring to the boil (the heat will release the juices from the fruit), lower the heat and gently simmer for 30 minutes, stirring occasionally until thick and pulpy.

Remove from heat and leave to cool. Store in an airtight glass jar in the fridge. Keeps for about a week.

163

Orange-kissed Seed Crackers

60 g (2 oz/½ cup) sunflower seeds
60 g (2 oz/½ cup) sesame seeds
40g (1½ oz/⅓ cup) linseed (flaxseeds), ground
60 g (2 oz/½ cup) hemp seeds
100 g (3½ oz/scant 1 cup) amaranth flour (or quinoa flour or almond flour)
1½ tsp sea salt
60 ml (2 fl oz/¼ cup) olive oil
2 tbsp orange juice
1 tbsp clear honey, use maple syrup if you are vegan

Makes about 20

These gluten-free and nut-free multi-seed crackers are almost too easy to make – no kneading or leavening needed. Just stir the ingredients together, flatten out on a tray and bake. You will end up with delicious crispy crackers that are great with any of the spreads in this chapter. If you can't find hemp seeds increase the amount of sunflower seeds. If you like your seeds natural omit the orange juice and honey.

Preheat the oven to 150°C (300°F/Gas 2).

Reserve a quarter of the seeds for topping then mix all the ingredients, except the orange juice and honey, with 300 ml (10 fl oz/1¼ cups) water, using a wooden spoon in a medium-sized bowl. You should have a loose batter. If it is not loose enough, add some more water; it will evaporate as you bake the crackers.

Line two 30 x 35 cm (12 x 14 in) baking trays with baking paper and pour the batter on. Use a spatula to flatten it out as thinly as you can. Bake in the oven for 25 minutes.

Meanwhile, whisk together the honey and orange juice in a small bowl. Remove the trays from the oven, brush the crackers with the orange glaze and sprinkle with the remaining seeds. Cut into 5 cm (2 in) pieces and bake for 30 minutes more or until they are crunchy. Cool on a wire rack.

Sprout Ceviche

grated zest and juice of 3 limes
1 shallot, finely chopped
2 tbsp extra virgin olive oil
½ tsp sea salt
½ tsp fresh red chilli, seeded and finely
    chopped
1 large handful of coriander
    (cilantro) leaves
200 g (7 oz/2¼ cups) sprouted mung
    beans (see page 28), or use bought

Serves 4

Even though we don't eat fish at home, we love marinating all kinds of vegetables in fresh ceviche flavours. It can be anything from a more complex ceviche salad to a simple side dish, like this one. Sprouts work particularly well with so much dressing, as they soak up the flavours. If making this for a buffet, it would look pretty to serve a spoonful of sprouts in endive leaves. Or just scoop a spoonful onto your plate as a side dish.

Put the lime zest and juice, onion, olive oil, salt and chilli in a mixing bowl and stir to combine. Add the sprouts and coriander and give it another stir. Leave for 15 minutes before serving to intensify the flavours.

Tip: Try using fresh green peas, shredded cucumber, fresh corn or alfalfa sprouts instead of mung bean sprouts.

SMALL BITES

Courgette Rolls with Passion Fruit & Lemon Ricotta

2 courgettes (zucchini)
2 tsp sea salt
250 g (9 oz/1 cup) ricotta cheese
5 passion fruit (or about 100 ml/½ cup
thawed pulp if using frozen)
juice of ½ a lemon
1 handful of basil leaves,
coarsely chopped
freshly ground black pepper

Makes about 12 rolls

If you have been reading and trying a few of our recipes, you might have noticed our slight obsession with lemon. Whenever we feel that something is missing in a recipe, we tend to reach for a lemon. Lemon pairs particularly well with ricotta, but, then again, we think it tastes great with almost anything. These rolls looks pretty impressive on a buffet table, but are surprisingly simple to do. If you can't find passion fruits use frozen pulp or finely chopped mango.

Thinly slice the courgettes lengthwise, about 6 mm (¼ in) thick. Place in a large colander, sprinkle with the salt and toss well. Set aside to drain for 30 minutes. Rinse well.

Transfer the courgettes to a clean tea towel, pat dry and brush the cut sides with olive oil. Heat a chargrill pan on medium-high heat and griddle the slices for 4 minutes on each side, or until tender and grill marks appear. Set aside to cool.

Put the ricotta in a mixing bowl. Cut the passion fruits in half and scoop out the seeds and pulp of 3 of them into the mixing bowl. Add the lemon juice, basil, salt and pepper and mix everything together.

Put 1 tablespoon of the ricotta mixture at the end of each courgette slice. Roll up and place on a serving plate. Repeat with the remaining slices. Top with seeds and pulp from the remaining passion fruits.

Red Pepper & Rosemary Spread

3 large red (bell) peppers, halved and
  seeded
75 g (2½ oz / ⅔ cup) sunflower seeds
a pinch of cayenne
sea salt
juice of ½ a lemon
2 sprigs of rosemary, leaves picked

Makes about 250 g (9 oz/1 cup)

When roasted, the peppers lose all their strength and acidity and take on a very round, almost smoked flavour, which pairs well with toasted sunflower seeds and a hint of cayenne. Although good on a sandwich, this spread has far more uses than that. It magically pairs with almost anything savoury that we make, so it is one of the jars in our fridge that always goes from full to empty in no time.

Preheat the oven to 200°C (400°F/Gas 6).

Prepare the peppers, place on a baking tray and roast for about 40 minutes, or until slightly charred. Remove from the oven and leave to cool.

Meanwhile, briefly toast the sunflower seeds, cayenne and salt in a frying pan. When the peppers are cold, peel the skin away. Chop them and place in a food processor or blender, add the sunflower seed, lemon juice and rosemary, and purée until smooth. Taste and adjust the seasoning if necessary. Transfer to an airtight glass jar. Keeps in the fridge for up to 2 weeks.

Sage & Walnut Pâté

200 g (7oz/1 cup) sundried tomatoes in
   oil (15–20), drained (if not in oil,
   soak them in water until soft)
200 g (7 oz/2 cups) walnuts, soaked in
   cold water for 6–8 hours or overnight
10 sage leaves, chopped
sea salt and freshly ground pepper

Makes about 400 g (14 oz/2 cups)

It's not often that we envy meat-
eaters, but when it comes to things
to put on bread, vegetarian options
are much more limited (unless you
like fake ham). Sure, we have cheese,
fruit compote and peanut butter. But
we sometimes crave something more
savoury, so then we make this pâté.
It's great on a piece of Dark Danish
Rye Bread (see page 58) or Swedish
Crispbread (see page 48).

Place all the ingredients with 2 tbsp water in a food processor or use
an immersion / hand blender. Mix until smooth. Add a little more water
if necessary to form a thick paste. Transfer to airtight glass jars. Keeps
in the fridge for about a week.

Broccoli Pesto

1 large head of broccoli, florets
and stems chopped
3 sprigs of basil or sage, leaves
picked
juice of ½ a lemon
80 g (3 oz/¾ cup) hazelnuts
(or toasted chickpeas)

2 garlic cloves, peeled
120 ml (4 fl oz/½ cup) extra virgin olive oil
sea salt and freshly ground black pepper

Makes about 500 g (1 lb 2 oz/2 cups)

Broccoli is one of those vegetables that most people want to cook, but we actually prefer it raw.
This recipe and the Broccoli Salad with Pomegranates & Raisins (see page 68) are two examples of how good it can be. We have omitted the cheese usually found in pestos, but if you are not vegan, a few slices of pecorino work great here.

Place all the ingredients in a blender or food processor with 2 tbsp water and purée until smooth, stopping and scraping down sides as necessary. Taste and adjust the seasoning. Add more olive oil or water if it feels too dry and more nuts or chickpeas if it is too runny. Transfer to airtight glass jars. Keeps in the fridge for a few days. Serve as a spread or with pasta.

Crunchy Curried Egg Salad

6 eggs (at room temperature)
a small handful of pumpkin seeds,
    toasted
1 red apple, halved, cored and
    cut into 1 cm (½ in) cubes
10 radishes, thinly sliced
5 sticks asparagus spears, cut
    into 1 cm (½ in) pieces
1 large bunch of chives, snipped
    (reserve a few for serving), including
    flowers when in season

FOR THE DRESSING
    120 ml (4 fl oz/½ cup) plain yoghurt
    2 tbsp mayonnaise, optional
    1 tsp ground curry powder
        (or more to taste)
    a pinch of cayenne
    sea salt

Serves 4

*Egg salad is an essential topping on
the Danish open rye sandwiches
called* smørrebrød. *It's traditionally
quite heavy, so we usually make a
lighter version using yoghurt, crunchy
fruit and vegetables. Serve on top
of some Dark Danish Rye Bread
(see page 58).*

Place the eggs (using a spoon!) into a pan of boiling water. Lower the
heat to medium and gently boil for 7–8 minutes. Toast the pumpkin
seeds in a frying pan.

Prepare the curry dressing by whisking all ingredients together in a small
bowl and set aside.

Remove the eggs from the heat and place the pan under running water.
When the eggs have cooled, crack and peel each egg and chop into 1 cm
(½ in) cubes. Put into a bowl with the other ingredients. Stir gently
with a large spoon (you don't want to mash the eggs) so all ingredients
are well coated in curry dressing. Put a nice handful of chives on top
and serve.

SMALL BITES

Spicy Skinny Root Sticks

500 g (1 lb 2oz) roots, such as carrots,
   sweet potatoes, parsnip, turnip
2 tbsp olive oil
a pinch chilli powder, or more to taste
1 tsp sea salt

Serves 4

We don't eat a lot of French fries at home, but that will hardly come as a surprise. However, when we do, we often make these instead of the traditional deep-fried version. They are perfectly crisp and crunchy, even though they are only baked – all thanks to how thinly they are sliced. Great served with our Portobello & Peach Burgers (see page 118).

Preheat the oven to 200°C (400°F/Gas 6).

Wash and peel the roots, or leave the skins on for a crunchier texture. Slice them into 3 mm (⅛ in) thin slices, lengthwise, then stack the slices and cut them into 3 mm (⅛ in) thin sticks. Pat dry using paper towels and place in a mixing bowl.

Add the olive oil, chilli powder and salt and toss so every single stick is coated. Place the root sticks on two baking trays lined with baking paper. Make sure you spread them out in one layer. Bake for about 8 minutes, or until golden with crisp, brown ends. Since we use different roots, the baking time can vary slightly. Keep an eye on the oven, and remove any that are already done.

Drinks

'My favourite drink? Ha, that's easy! The drips of a sweet Sicilian blood orange, squeezed into a glass. I can't think of anything better. No, wait. Two Swedish apples, from your aunt's tree, pushed through our juicer together with a knob of ginger. That is my favourite drink. No, no, now I know, the simple cane juice we were served on that street in Saigon, th...'
'Well, there you have it,' David interrupts me.

I asked him how I should start this chapter. And he has got a point; I have a drinking problem. I love all the possibilities that come from mixing fresh fruit and vegetables into juices, smoothies, shakes and lassis. No wonder we have worn out three blenders and one juice machine in three years.

We make juices for breakfast, juices for sweetening food and desserts, and juices to use in smoothies. You can turn an unexpected vegetable like broccoli, into the most delicious drink, just by balancing its flavours with a little sweet and some tanginess. Apple, lemon and ginger usually do the trick. In this chapter we have rounded up a few of our best juice and smoothie recipes. And we have included an alcohol-free cocktail, an elderflower lemonade and two Indian drinks, one warm and one cold.

– *Luise*

Bubbling Kombucha Cocktail

FOR THE COCKTAIL
- 250 ml (8½ fl oz/1 cup) Kombucha brew, homemade or ready-made
- 250 ml (8½ fl oz/1 cup) apple juice, unsweetened
- 120 ml (4 fl oz/½ cup) crushed ice
- 2 thinly sliced rhubarb sticks

FOR THE KOMBUCHA
- 80 g (3 oz/⅓ cup) sugar (we use brown)
- 2 green or black teabags
- 1 Kombucha 'mushroom' + 120 ml (4 fl oz/½ cup) liquid culture (it will come with the mushroom)

Serves 2

Kombucha is a fermented, enzyme- and probiotic-rich tea, which you either can make yourself or buy pre-made in health food stores. You can drink it as it is, add to smoothies or even make into ice lollies. We love the festive bubbles you find naturally in Kombucha. They are perfect in a fruity, alcohol-free summer cocktail. If you do not start a new batch right away, you need to rinse out the mushroom jars every 4 weeks. Just put the mushroom and culture into a bowl while rinsing the jars with hot water, and then pour them back into their jars. Store at room temperature.

FOR THE KOMBUCHA

Boil 1 litre (34 fl oz/4¼ cups) water and let it cool slightly. Pour into a large glass jar, add the sugar and stir until it has dissolved. Add the tea and steep for 15 minutes.

Remove the teabags and let the mixture cool to 25°C (75°F). It is important to measure the temperature – if it is too hot you will kill the mushroom. Place the Kombucha mushroom and culture in the cooled tea mixture, cover with muslin, secure with the rubber band and keep in a warm room (temperature around 23–25°C/75–80°F) for 8–14 days. By this time it will probably have produced a baby mushroom on the surface, small bubbles will start to show and the liquid will taste vinegary. If it is still very sweet, leave it for another week or so.

When ready, remove the baby mushroom and the mother mushroom using a wooden or plastic spoon (do not use metal), and rinse under lukewarm water. Place each mushroom in a separate glass jar together with half a cup of the Kombucha culture (the one you just made) and cover. Pour your newly brewed Kombucha into bottles and store in the fridge for up to one month.

To make the cocktail, mix the measured Kombucha and apple juice in a large jug with the ice. Crush half the rhubarb slices with the back of a knife. Stir all into the jug and serve straight away.

185

Chocolate & Blackberry Milkshake

15 fresh blackberries
   (or thawed if frozen)
2 frozen bananas (or fresh bananas
   and 2 ice cubes)
250 ml (8 ½ fl oz/1 cup) coconut milk
120 ml (4 fl oz/½ cup) almond milk or
   milk of your choice
3 tbsp cacao powder
1 tbsp cacao nibs, optional
1 tbsp Nut Butter (see page 27)

Makes 2 glasses

We couldn't write this book without including a milkshake. It wouldn't feel right. This chocolate version is made with coconut milk, which gives it a rich and creamy texture. We love making layered milkshakes and smoothies. They look prettier and make the drinking experience more interesting as the separate flavours slowly combine when you work your way down the shake. Blackberries and chocolate are perfect together, but raspberries would be really good as well.

Divide the blackberries between two glasses. Muddle them (mash them gently) in the bottom of the glasses. You can use a pestle or end of a rolling pin to do this. Put the rest of the ingredients in a blender and run on high-speed until frothy. Pour carefully into the glasses, make sure the blackberries stay on the bottom, and serve immediately.

Tip: We often peel and slice ripe, leftover bananas and store them in a container in the freezer. They are great for making smoothies, and you don't need to add any ice.

Juicing

If you have never tried making your own juice, you are in for a real treat. Although you can make juice with a blender, we recommend using a juice machine for the best results. You can juice most vegetables and it's a great way to increase your intake of vitamins and minerals.
Since not all vegetables taste great as they are, we usually add some tanginess and sweetness. Lemon adds a fresh flavour to green vegetables like kale, broccoli and spinach. The vitamin C also improves the body's ability to absorb the iron in those vegetables. Apple is one of the best fruits to juice. It has a very sweet flavour and releases a lot of juice.

Each serves 2

Choose a few fruit and veg from each group you will get a good and balanced juice:

Vegetables:
  kale, broccoli, spinach, beetroot (red beets), carrot, fennel, bell pepper, cucumber, tomato, cauliflower, sweet potato, romaine, celery
Sweet fruits:
  apple, pear, melon, peach, plum, orange, cherries
Tangy fruits:
  lemon, grapefruit, lime, kiwi fruit
Herbs:
  parsley, basil, lemon balm, mint
For a kick:
  ginger, horseradish, wheatgrass, liquorice, turmeric, saffron

Virgin Apple Mojito

3 limes, chopped
10–15 mint leaves
1 apple
2 kiwi
250 ml (8 ½ fl oz/1 cup) soda water

Put the limes and mint into the glasses and muddle (lightly crush) with a pestle. Press the apples and kiwi fruits through a juice machine, then add the soda water. Serve in glasses with a few ice cubes and straws.

Beetroot & Watermelon Juice

2 medium beetroot (red beet)
½ small watermelon
1 handful of fresh mint, leaves picked

Press the ingredients through a juice machine. Serve in glasses with a few ice cubes a and straw in each.

Tips:
- Depending on the quality of your machine, leaf and grass vegetables can be a little tricky to juice. A good tip is to roll them into a tight ball before adding them to the juicer.
- If you do not have a juicer, use a blender and strain the juice through a nut milk bag, cheesecloth or a fine sieve.
- If you find a combination that you like, turn it into a smoothie by adding milk, avocado, yoghurt, banana, mango or frozen berries.
- You can easily make juices and smoothies into ice lollies (popsicles). Pour the mixture into lolly moulds, place a stick in each and freeze.

Carrot & Grapefruit Juice

3 carrots
1 grapefruit
1 cm (½ in) piece of fresh ginger
1 eating apple
½ yellow (bell) pepper, seeded

Press the ingredients through a juice machine.
Serve in glasses with a few ice cubes and a straw in each.

Raspberry & Liquorice Juice

2 eating apples
150 g (5 oz/1¼ cup) raspberries
  (thawed if frozen)
1 tsp liquorice powder (add after juicing)

Press the apples and raspberries through a juice machine.
Add the liquorice powder and stir. Serve in glasses with
a few ice cubes and a straw in each.

Green Cleanse Power Shot

2 eating apples
1 cm (½ in) piece of fresh ginger
1 lemon
½ fennel bulb
1 tsp wheatgrass powder
a pinch of ground turmeric

Press the apples, ginger, lemon and fennel through a juice machine.
Stir in the wheatgrass powder and turmeric. Serve in glasses with
a few ice cubes and a straw in each.

Sweet Hazelnut Masala Chai

2 cinnamon sticks
6 cloves
6 cardamom pod, split
2 star anise
1 slice of fresh ginger
2 tbsp black or green tea leaves
1–2 tbsp palm sugar
250 ml (8½ fl oz/1 cup) Hazelnut or
   Almond Milk (see page 27),
   or use bought

Serves 4

This hot tea is all about flavours. We love how the scent of cinnamon, star anise, cardamom and clove fills our kitchen as the chai simmers on the stove. We make it with our own hazelnut milk, and it is just as good on a hot summer day as a dark and cold winter evening.

Put (250 ml/8½ fl oz/1 cup) water and the spices in a saucepan and gently bring to a boil, then reduce the heat and simmer for 15 minutes. Remove from the heat, add the tea and coconut palm sugar and steep for 5–7 minutes. Strain out the spices and tea and stir. Add the nut milk, reheat until barely simmering, then pour into cups and serve.

Smoothies

As we mentioned earlier, we make smoothies almost every day.
They are different depending on the season and what we have in
our fridge, freezer and fruit basket. Here are two different versions.
The Wake-up Smoothie is quite elaborate, while the Classic Berry
Smoothie is simpler. We vary it by adding superfood powders, seeds,
nuts, pea or hemp protein powder and herbs.

Each serves 2

Wake-up Smoothie

½ pineapple
½ tsp green tea powder (instant)
5 broccoli florets
a handful of parsley
1 cm (½ in) piece of fresh ginger, peeled
250 ml (8½ fl oz/1 cup) unsweetened apple juice or water
  (depending on how sweet you prefer it)
3 ice cubes

Put all the ingredients in a blender and blend until nice and smooth. Pour into 2 glasses and serve immediately.

Classic Berry Smoothie

125 g (4 oz/1 cup) fresh berries (thawed if frozen)
4 tbsp dried goji berries
1 banana
350 ml (12 fl oz/1½ cups) oat milk (or milk of your choice)
1 tsp vanilla extract

Put all the ingredients in a blender and blend until nice and smooth; add extra milk if you prefer it thinner. Pour into 2 glasses and serve immediately.

Saffron, Rosehip & Honey Lassi

350 ml (12 fl oz/1½ cups) yoghurt
2 tbsp clear honey
2 tsp rosehip powder (or ½ tsp ground cinnamon)
1 tsp bee pollen (optional)
½ tsp freshly ground cardamom seeds
2 pinches of saffron powder
a pinch of salt
2 ice cubes

Serves 2

In India they often drink lassi to accompany a meal. It's easy to understand why, since it's exactly what you need after a spicy curry. When we travelled around in India we tried at least a dozen different versions. Apart from the traditional salted lassi and smoothie-like fruit lassis, they also use more complex flavours like rose water, honey or saffron. We have combined a few of those flavours in our version. You can buy rosehip powder in most health food stores, if you can't find it you could leave it out or use cinnamon instead.

Combine all the ingredients in a blender with 120 ml (4 fl oz/1½ cups) water. Pulse until smooth, light and frothy. Taste and add more saffron if necessary. Pour into 2 large glasses and serve immediately.

Elderflower Lemonade

40 elderflower heads
3 lemons
240 ml (8 fl oz/1 cup) clear honey

Makes 2 litres (68 fl oz/8½ cups) lemonade

Elderflower has the most wonderful aroma. During spring, the blossoming trees can be found everywhere around Stockholm – you can easily find a tree just by closing your eyes and following the scent. We don't, however, recommend picking elderflowers in very urban areas. Search outside the city if you can.

It has always been a mystery to us why all recipes drench the elderflowers' wonderful flavour in sugar. There is no need for such absurd quantities. Our lemonade is therefore half as sweet, but twice as flavourful.

Gently shake the elderflowers to get rid of any small bugs or dirt. Cut the lemons into thin slices. In a wide, large pan or bucket (crock), arrange the elderflowers and lemon slices in layers. Bring 2 litres (68 fl oz/8½ cups) water to a boil in a large saucepan. Add honey and stir until dissolved, then pour over the elderflowers and lemon. Leave to steep in a cool place for 48 hours, stirring once a day. Steep for longer, if you prefer a more concentrated flavour.

Strain the liquid by pouring it through a cheesecloth or muslin into a large bowl. Pour through a funnel into clean bottles and refrigerate. Will keep for at least a few weeks unopened. Serve with sparkling water, according to taste.

Tip: You can freeze the flowers and add to smoothies, or make more lemonade, off season.

Sweets & Treats

I have this strange habit, which I don't even think about, but drives Luise crazy. Apparently I always leave a small piece of whatever I cook/bake/eat behind. It can be two spoonfuls of salad in a bowl, four strawberries in the box, or a tablespoon of flour in the bag when I am baking. My own theory is that I think it is good to save it for later. But truth be told, we only end up with ridiculously small portions of leftovers, and half empty bags of flour in the pantry. Hopefully, if you try any of the sweets and treats in this chapter, there will be no leftovers. Our fingers are crossed that you and your family will lick the bowls, ask for second servings, and reach for the last piece.

All our desserts are sweetened with natural sweeteners, baked with whole grains, and here and there we have even added some vegetables to them. Our intention has never been to make anything less indulgent than you are used to. In our opinion, a cake that combines the subtle aroma of a beetroot, with dark decadent chocolate, the soft texture of spelt flour and the toasty tones from maple syrup, is far more intriguing than any sugar and flour cake on the market. We are all about natural flavours and hope we can get you hooked, whether you are trying our cold berry soup, cardamom flavoured buns or double chocolate raspberry brownies.

– *David*

Cardamom & Apple Buns

1 tbsp fast-action dried yeast
½ tbsp cardamom seeds,
  freshly ground
a pinch of sea salt
50 g (1¾ oz) unsalted butter or coconut oil
250 ml (8½ fl oz/1 cup) soya milk
  (or milk of your choice)
5 tbsp clear honey or maple syrup
250 g (9 oz/2 cups) light spelt flour
150 g (5 oz/1 cup) wholegrain
  spelt flour

FILLING
50 g (2 oz/½ stick) unsalted butter,
  at room temperature or coconut oil
120 ml (4 fl oz/½ cup) applesauce,
  unsweetened
1 eating apple, grated, excess
  moisture squeezed out
2 tbsp desiccated coconut
½ tbsp cardamom seeds, freshly
  ground
beaten egg to glaze

Makes around 15 buns

I remember my grandmother standing in her farm kitchen with a rolling pin in her hand and a double batch of cinnamon buns ready to be rolled out on a floured table. I also remember eating those buns hot from the oven. Not much could make a 6-year-old boy happier. We finally came up with a bun recipe that had all the same qualities – this is a healthier recipe of the traditional cardamom buns. Since these buns aren't super-sweet, we added more filling to compensate. We also updated the flavours by adding apple, coconut and freshly ground cardamom. If you make these, you have to eat the first bun hot from the oven. There is nothing quite like it.
– David

Stir the yeast, cardamom and salt in a large bowl and set aside. Melt the butter in a saucepan, add the milk and honey and heat until the temperature is about 40°C (100°F). Pour over the yeast and stir until dissolved.

Sift the flours together and add about two-thirds of it to the yeast and milk mixture. Mix to a dough. Gradually knead in enough of the remaining flour just until soft and no longer sticky. Do not over-knead. Cover and leave to rise in a warm place for about an hour, or until double in bulk.

On a floured surface roll and stretch the dough to a rectangle, about 50 x 45 cm (20 x 18 in) wide and about 5 mm (¼ in) thick.

Spread the butter and applesauce evenly across the whole dough and sprinkle on the apple shreds, coconut and cardamom. Carefully lift one third of the dough (closest to you) and fold it two-thirds of the way up, then fold down the top third. Now you should have a rectangle that is roughly 50 x 15 cm (20 x 6 in). Use a sharp knife to cut the dough into roughly 3 cm (1¼ in) wide strips.

Take each strip and carefully (so the filling doesn't fall out) stretch and twist them three times and tie into loose knot-shaped buns, with the ends tucked into the middle. Put on a baking tray lined with baking paper, cover with kitchen towel, and leave to rise for 30 minutes.

Pre-heat the oven to 220°C (425°F/Gas 7). Brush the buns with a beaten egg and bake for 10–12 minutes, until golden.

SWEETS AND TREATS

Decadent Beetroot & Chocolate Cake

150 ml (5 fl oz/⅔ cup) extra virgin olive oil
120 ml (4 fl oz/⅓ cup) maple syrup or clear honey
50 g (2 oz/⅓ cup) dark chocolate (75% cocoa solids) broken into pieces
250 g (9 oz/scant 2 cups) raw beetroot (red beets) or about 3–4 medium sized, grated

3 eggs
200 g (7 oz/scant 1¾ cups) light spelt flour
2 tsp baking powder
5 tbsp cacao powder
a pinch of sea salt
1 tbsp desiccated coconut

Serves 10

I have been baking chocolate cakes since I was a teenager. In fact, for a few years I solemnly baked chocolate cakes two or three times a week, so I see myself as pretty experienced in this area. Although this cake is far less sweetened than my teenage chocolate cakes, it has so much more flavour. Don't be intimidated by the beetroots. They don't taste strange at all; instead they actually add a depth to the chocolate.

– David

Preheat the oven to 180°C (350°F/Gas 4).

Warm the oil in a saucepan on a very low heat. Add the maple syrup and chocolate and stir until the chocolate is melted. Remove from heat. Add the grated beetroot and stir to combine. Beat the eggs in a small bowl and add them to the saucepan.

In a separate bowl, sift the flour, baking powder, cacao powder and salt together and stir into the beet mixture.

Grease a 20 cm (10 in) bundt pan or a cake tin with a little oil. Sprinkle the sides of the pan with shredded coconut, to prevent the batter from sticking. Pour in the cake batter and bake for 25–30 minutes, or until slightly dark and cracked on top and still a little sticky inside.

Leave to cool for 15 minutes before carefully removing the cake from the tin. It tastes amazing while warm, but can be cooled and kept in the fridge for 2–3 days.

Carrot, Coconut & Banana Cupcakes

80 g (3 oz/⅓ cup) unsalted butter
4 tbsp maple syrup or agave syrup
1 tsp cardamom seeds, freshly ground
1 tsp ground cinnamon
1 tsp ground allspice
½ vanilla bean or ½ tsp vanilla extract
150 g (5 oz/1½ cups) almonds, ground
60 g (2 oz/½ cup) besan flour (chickpea flour) or another gluten-free flour
50 g (2 oz/½ cup) desiccated coconut
2 tsp baking powder
200 g (7 oz/1⅓ cups) carrots (about 4), grated

1 large ripe banana
4 egg whites

FROSTING

200 g (7 oz/scant 1 cup) cream cheese
3 tbsp clear honey
juice of ½ a lime
15 hazelnuts, coarsely chopped

Makes about 12 cupcakes

These cupcakes are filled with wonderful warm spices. The scent of cardamom, cinnamon and allspice oozes from them as they come fresh from the oven. We only use egg whites and not very much flour in this recipe, which makes them very light and airy. Muffins and cupcakes always taste best eaten fresh. If you are having a party you can of course make them a day in advance, but nothing beats the taste when they are fresh from the oven.

Preheat the oven to 180°C (350°F/Gas 4). Line a muffin tray with 12 paper cases.

Melt the butter on a low heat in a small saucepan. Add the maple syrup and all the spices and stir well. Set aside to infuse for 10 minutes.

Put the almonds in a mixing bowl and add the besan flour, coconut and baking powder.

Put the grated carrots and banana in the blender and whizz until the banana is completely mashed and incorporated with the carrots (you can also do this step by hand). Add to the mixing bowl and stir well to combine with the dry ingredients.

Beat the egg whites until softly peaking. Fold into the cupcake mixture and then add the spice-infused butter and stir until smooth. Spoon into the muffin cases and bake for 25–30 minutes or until golden.

Meanwhile, make the frosting. Whisk together the cream cheese, honey and lime juice in a small bowl.

Let the muffins cool on a wire rack before spooning or piping on the frosting. Decorate with coarsely chopped hazelnuts.

Simple Chocolate Mousse

2 ripe avocados, halved, stoned and peeled
3 ripe bananas
80 g (30 oz/⅓ cup) Nut Butter (see page 27)
30 g (1 oz/¼ cup) cacao powder
2 tbsp carob powder (or more
   cacao)
2 tbsp hemp seeds, optional
a pinch of sea salt
fresh berries, to serve

Serves 4

This vegan chocolate mousse is pretty far from the traditional kind. First of all, it is ridiculously simple, taking no more than 3 minutes to make. None of the common ingredients (heavy cream, chocolate, eggs, butter) are used – instead the creaminess and sweetness come from avocado and banana and the flavour from nut butter and cacao powder. We usually use almond butter, but when we don't have it at home we also use peanut butter or hazelnut butter.

Put all ingredients in a blender or food processor. Puree for about 30 seconds or until it reaches a mousse-like consistency. Scoop into glasses or small coffee cups and put in the fridge for 30 minutes. Serve topped with fresh berries.

Tip: Cacao and carob powder complete eachother, both in taste and nutritional values. Cacao is rich in magnesium and carob is rich in calcium.

SWEETS AND TREATS

Double Chocolate Raspberry Brownie

25 fresh medjool dates, pitted
60 ml (2 fl oz/¼ cup) coconut oil
2 tbsp maple syrup
40 g (1½ oz/⅓ cup) cacao powder
2 tea bags of raspberry leaf herbal tea
   (we use Clipper or Yogi), cut open
½ tsp sea salt
150 g (5 oz/1¼ cups) coarsely
   chopped walnuts

CHOCOLATE TOPPING
60 ml (2 fl oz/¼ cup) soft coconut oil
2 tbsp maple syrup
40 g (1½ oz/⅓ cup) cacao powder

Fresh raspberries, to serve

Serves 6

This is a dressed-up alternative to our Spirulina Chocolate Truffles (see page 232). Although delicious as a treat, those truffles might not be pretty enough to qualify as a dessert after dinner. Therefore we created this more elaborate version with a raspberry leaf flavour and melted chocolate topping. We also do a winter version of this by substituting the raspberry leaf tea with chai tea.

Grease six 10 cm (4 in) spring-form cake tins or one large 23cm (9 in) spring form cake tin with coconut oil.

Purée all the brownie ingredients, except the walnuts, in a food processor with 2 tbsp water. If your food processor isn't powerful enough to puree all the ingredients at the same time, you can divide it into three different batches and then combine them afterwards.

Add the nuts and combine the mixture by hand. Divide the mixture between the cake tins (or put it into the large tin). Rub a little coconut oil on your hands to prevent the mixture from sticking, then use your fingers to flatten out the mixture in the tins. It should be about 1 cm (½ in) deep. Put the tins in the fridge and leave to set for a least 30 minutes. If covered, they will keep in the fridge for a couple of days.

At the end of the chilling time, start making the chocolate topping. Melt the coconut oil and maple syrup on low heat in a small saucepan. Add the cacao powder while stirring.

Remove the brownies from the fridge. Pour the chocolate topping over and serve immediately, so your guests can watch the chocolate as it sets. It usually takes about 2 minutes. Top with a few raspberries, carefully remove from the spring-form tins and, well, dig in!

Tip: We often use herbal teas instead of spices when we need flavours that can be a bit tricky to find. Chamomile, chai, peppermint and rosehip are herbal teas that add interesting flavours to desserts, soups and breads.

Frozen Strawberry Cheesecake on a Sunflower Crust

300 g (10½ oz/2½ cups) sunflower
    seeds
2 tbsp hemp seeds, optional
12 fresh medjool dates, pitted
2 tbsp coconut oil
½ tsp sea salt

FILLING
    300 g (10½ oz/2 cups) fresh
        strawberries (or frozen unsweetened
        strawberries)
    juice of ½ a lemon
    120 ml (4 fl oz/½ cup) clear honey
        or agave syrup

500 g (2 oz/2 cups) quark
    (or Greek yoghurt or mascarpone)

TOPPING
    250 g (9oz/1 cup) strawberries
    a few edible flowers (see tip)

Serves 8–10

*I don't think we have ever served
this cake to someone who hasn't
immediately loved it. Therefore it has
become one of our go-to recipes for all
kinds of occasions. We used to make it
with nuts in the crust, but lately we
have moved to this seed-based crust.
It has the most wonderful flavour
and texture, not to mention that it is
allergy friendly and gluten-free.
Since the crust is very sweet, the filling
doesn't have to be. If you are looking
for new variations, you can play
around with all kinds of yoghurts, soft
cheeses or coconut creams. You can
also vary the colour of the filling by
adding different berries to it. If you
are having a big party make a range:
blueberry blue, kiwi green, mango
yellow and so on …*

Toast the sunflower seeds in a frying pan on low heat, or on a baking
tray on 180°C (350°F/Gas 4), for 6–8 minutes. Let cool for a few
minutes before putting them into a food processor or blender together
with the hemp seeds. Pulse for about 20 seconds. The seeds should be
chopped but not powdered.

Add the dates, coconut oil and salt and process until the mixture comes
together to a sticky crust. Alternatively, mash the dates until caramel-
smooth and work in its remaining ingredients. Put the mixture into a
20 cm (8 in) spring-form cake tin and flatten it out over the base. Chill
in the fridge while you prepare the filling.

Purée the strawberries, lemon juice and honey in a food processor or
blender, pour into a large bowl and add the quark. Mix well. Pour the
mixture on top of the crust in the cake tin and put it in the freezer for
about 1½ hours. You can keep it in the freezer for a few days but you
will need to let it thaw for about 20 minutes before serving.

Top the cake with strawberries and a couple of flowers.
Serve immediately.

Tip: Here are some suggestions for edible flowers: violas, calendula,
roses, rosehip, dandelions, carnations, lavender, cornflowers, pea
flowers, day lilies and chamomile. Although the flowers are edible
we mainly use them for decoration.

Tip: For vegans substitute vegan cream cheese for quark.

SWEETS AND TREATS

Fruit Roll-Ups

RED RASPBERRY ROLLS
  300 g (10½ oz/2½ cups) raspberries,
    fresh, thawed or frozen
  1 banana
  1 tbsp unsweetened applesauce

YELLOW MANGO ROLLS
  1 large mango
  2 oranges
  10 dried, unsulphered apricots

Makes 1 tray/20 roll-ups

They look, feel and taste like sweets, but the only ingredient in our roll-ups is fruit. We have taken these to a couple of birthday parties for Elsa's friends and they have always been a success. Here are two recipes, but you can create endless colour and flavour combinations by changing the fruit. They need about 5–6 hours in the oven on the lowest temperature, so we usually make two or three batches at a time. If you have a dehydrator, now is the time to use it. Pour the puree onto your Teflex-lined dehydrator trays. Spread evenly until about 5 mm (¼ in) thick. Dehydrate for 6–7 hours at 45°C (115°F) or until it is completely dry. Peel off the Teflex.

Prepare the raspberry rolls. Add the fruit to a blender or food processor. Purée on high speed until smooth. Taste it and add more sweet fruit (applesauce or banana) if needed. Now check the consistency – you should be able to pour the purée, but it should be thick enough to stay where you pour it. Add some orange juice or water if it is too thick and more fruit if it is too thin.

Preheat the oven to its lowest setting. Line two baking trays with non-stick baking paper or silicone baking mats if you have one.

Pour the purée onto one of the trays – 500 ml (17 fl oz/2¼ cups) fruit purée should be enough to cover it. Spread it out evenly with a spatula – this is very important otherwise the rolls will end up too dry in one spot and too wet in another. It should be about 5 mm (¼ in) thick. Now prepare the mango rolls in the same way. Put in the oven. Open the oven door once an hour to let the moisture out and change position of the trays. They are ready when the puree isn't sticky anymore and can be separated from the baking paper, normally after 5–6 hours, depending on your oven.

We carefully remove them from the baking paper before cutting them, since we think it looks prettier, but you could also leave the paper on, and peel it off when you eat them. Use scissors or a sharp knife to cut them into 2.5 x 15 cm (1 x 6 in) strips and roll them up. Store in an airtight container in a cool place for up to a month.

Cantaloupe Granita with Lemon & Mint

1 kg (3 oz) cantaloupe melon
juice of ½ a lemon
120 ml (4 fl oz/½ cup) pure apple juice
  (or syrup, but then use less)
10 mint leaves

Serves 4–6

When I met David in Rome we often went out for a lemon granita. It is a typically Italian dessert that is very refreshing in the summer heat or after a heavy dinner. It is actually also easy to make yourself. You will need to whisk it into the right texture, but apart from that your freezer does all the work. And if you use seasonally sweet fruit, no sugar is needed.
– Luise

Cut the melon in half, discard the seeds and scoop out the flesh with a spoon. Put it into a blender or food processor, together with the rest of the ingredients. Pulse until everything is completely puréed. Taste it and make sure that the fruit is sweet enough. If not, add more apple juice. Pour into a shallow container, cover with a lid, and freeze. After about an hour it is time to open the lid and whisk the mixture with a fork. You want to break up any ice crystals that form. Put it back in the freezer. Whisk again every 30 minutes during the next 3 hours. Now it should have the typical granita texture and is ready to be served.
You can keep it in the freezer for a few days, but remember to check on it and every now and then and whisk with a fork, so it maintains the right texture.

Hemp Protein Bars

DRY MIXTURE
- 160 g (5½ oz/1 cup) pumpkin seeds
- 100 g (3½ oz/generous 1 cup) desiccated coconut
- 80 g (3 oz/½ cup) hemp seeds
- 50 g (2 oz/½ cup) hemp protein powder (or more hemp seeds)
- 50 g (2 oz/½ cup) chia seeds
- 2 tbsp bee pollen (optional), leave out if you are vegan

WET MIXTURE
- 20 fresh medjool dates, stoned
- 90 ml (3 fl oz/⅓ cup) coconut oil
- 30 g (1 oz/¼ cup) cacao powder
- 1 tsp vanilla extract

- 40 g (1½ oz/⅓ cup) rolled oats
- 2 tbsp poppy seeds

Makes around 15 bars

This is one of the most appreciated and commented recipes on our blog. The bars are not only really tasty as a midday snack for all ages, but we also wrap these in paper to eat after we have been working out. They are sweet in a very nice and nourishing way and packed with protein.

In a food processor or high-speed blender, pulse the dry ingredients quickly. Do not over-process, as you want it a little crunchy. Place the mixture in a bowl and set aside.

Add all the wet ingredients to the food processor or high-speed blender and purée. This might take some time. If your blender isn't powerful enough, you might have to help out by stirring around a few times with a fork or add a dash of water.

Pour the wet ingredients over the dry ingredients, add the oats and poppy seeds and stir until well combined.

Spread the batter into a 28 x 18 cm (11 x 7 in) baking tin lined with baking paper and press down the mixture so it is compact. Chill in the fridge for about 30 minutes.

Cut into bars, wrap them in paper and store in an airtight container. Keep for around a week in the fridge.

Tip: If you do not have a high-speed blender, place your pitted dates on a plate and mash with a fork until they are sticky and smooth as caramel, it'll take a few minutes. Then add the remaining ingredients one by one and knead by hand until well combined.

Vanilla Peaches with Pistachio Crumble

5 ripe peaches
4 tbsp dry vermouth
4 tbsp clear honey
1 vanilla pod
60 g (2 oz/⅓ cup) shelled pistachios,
  finely chopped
vanilla ice cream, yoghurt or
  mascarpone, to serve

Serves 5

When I was a kid my dad used to set bananas on fire in the frying pan by pouring alcohol on them. It was a little stunt he had and we were madly impressed every time. We asked him to do it often, even though we actually weren't too fond of the taste of the bananas. Today I have grown to love those flavours. I don't set my peaches on fire, but I think they make a pretty good dessert anyway.

– David

Preheat the oven to 200°C (400°F/Gas 6).

Cut each peach in half and remove the stone. Place the halves on a baking tray, cut side upwards.

Put the vermouth and honey in a small bowl. Cut the vanilla pod in half, scrape out the seeds and add to the bowl. Whisk until combined. Add the pistachios to the bowl and stir.

Scoop a teaspoon of the honey-drenched nuts into the pit of each peach. Drizzle the remaining vermouth mixture over the peaches, until they are all covered. Bake for about 20 minutes, or until very soft and slightly golden.

Serve with vanilla ice cream, yoghurt or mascarpone.

Cold Red Berry Soup with Cream

1 kg (3 oz) ripe red berries (such as
    strawberries, raspberries, redcurrants,
    lingonberries)
1 vanilla bean, seeds scraped (or 2 tsp
    vanilla extract)
25 fresh medjool dates, stoned
350 ml (12 fl oz/1½ cups) cream of your
    choice, for serving

Serves 4–6

Although David is pretty good at speaking Danish, there is one sentence he will never manage to pronounce like a true Dane. It's the name of this soup: Rødgrød med fløde. *It's just one of those impossible Danish sentences. The exact translation is actually red porridge with cream, but it is more like thick soup than porridge. Regardless of the name, it is the perfect summer treat on a hot day. Our version is quite different from the traditional, since we use the thickness of dates and the whole berries instead of adding sugar and starch.*
– Luise

Place the berries, vanilla and 250 ml (8½ fl oz/1 cup) water in a saucepan. Bring slowly to simmer on a low heat. Mash the pitted dates with a fork on a plate until smooth and add to the pan. Simmer for about 10 minutes – the berries and dates should almost have dissolved. Remove from the heat and mix the soup with a hand/immersion blender. Place a fine sieve over a large bowl in the sink. Pour the soup through it so all the seeds are strained. Use the back of a spoon to help the thick soup through. This takes a couple of minutes.
Place the soup in fridge for a few hours until completely cold.
Serve in deep plates or bowls with cream (oat, nut, coconut or cow's) drizzled on top.

Spirulina Chocolate Truffles

20 large fresh medjool dates, stoned
2 tbsp extra virgin coconut oil
2 tbsp desiccated coconut
2 tbsp cacao powder
1 tbsp spirulina powder or wheatgrass
 powder

ROLL IN
 10 almonds, coarsely chopped,
  or 3 tbsp desiccated coconut
  or 3 tbsp cacao powder

Serves 5

When we want a quick treat we often make raw truffles by blending fresh dates with nuts or seeds, various spices and cacao powder. It's a simple, no-fail recipe that we adjust to whatever we have in our pantry. They are perfect as an evening treat or a mid-day snack. Sometimes we also make them extra pretty by rolling them in different toppings, and give them as gifts. The rolling process is Elsa's favourite part.
Spirulina is a superfood that can be difficult to use because of its algae taste, but this recipe is so full of flavour that the nutritious spirulina just blends in.

Place the dates on a plate and mash with a fork until they are sticky and smooth as caramel. You can also use a food processor for this step. Add the rest of the ingredients and knead (or pulse) until mixed well. Place the mixture in the fridge for about 10 minutes.
Use your hands to form 15–20 round truffles; they should be half the size of a golf ball. Roll the truffles in chopped almonds, desiccated coconut or cacao powder and chill in the fridge for 20 minutes before serving.

233   SWEETS AND TREATS

Summer Berry Pancake Cake

PANCAKE BATTER
200 g (7 oz/1¾ cups) buckwheat flour
3 large eggs
480 ml (15 fl oz/2 cups) soy milk or milk of your choice
1 tbsp coconut oil, more for frying
a pinch of sea salt

LAYERS
3 ripe bananas, sliced thin
225 g (8 oz/2 cups) raspberries, mashed with a fork

225 g (8 oz/1½ cups) blackberries, mashed with a fork
125 g (4 oz/scant ⅔ cup) Nut Butter (see page 27)
120 ml (4 fl oz/½ cup) Raw Date Syrup (see page 30)
480 ml (15 fl oz/2 cups) thick cream (cow, oat or soya), chilled

TOPPING
150 g (5 oz/1¼ cups) raspberries
125 g (4 oz/1 cup) blackberries
2 tbsp chopped pistachio nuts

Serves 10

I have made different versions of this cake since I was a child, and I never get tired of it. I think it is so beautiful with all those stacks of pancakes, and the berries and cream squishing out from the sides. Traditionally you put jam between the layers, but we stick to fresh fruit, nut butter and date syrup. The pancakes should be very thin, so we always use a non-stick frying pan when we make these. You can prepare the pancakes one day in advance and assemble the cake just before serving.
– David

To make the batter, add all the ingredients, plus 240ml (8 fl oz/ 1 cup) water to a large mixing bowl and whisk vigorously until you have a smooth batter. Make sure that there are no lumps of flour left. Refrigerate for 20 minutes. Give it a good whisk after you have removed it from the fridge, as the flour tends to sink to the bottom.

Heat a 20 cm (8 in), preferably non-stick, frying pan on medium-high heat. When the pan is hot, add a few drops of oil and about 75 ml (2½ fl oz/ ⅓ cup) of the batter. Tilt the pan until the batter is evenly distributed. Fry for 45–60 seconds on each side, until the pancakes are golden and can be flipped easily with a spatula. Fry all of the pancakes – the batter should make about 15 – and place on baking paper to cool off. You can layer with baking paper between the pancakes to stop them sticking together.

To assemble, pour the cold cream into a large chilled bowl. Use an electric hand mixer or a whisk to whip it until soft peaks form. Set aside. Put the cold first pancake on a cake stand. Spread a layer of thin slices of banana evenly over the top. Add another pancake and top it with about a third of the mashed raspberries. Then continue with next pancake anda third of the mashed blackberries. Continue with another pancake and carefully spread a thin layer of nut butter and date syrup on it. Add another pancake and spread with a layer of whipped cream. Then start all over with the banana layer. Continue until all the pancakes are covered. Top with whipped cream, fresh fruit and finely chopped pistachios.

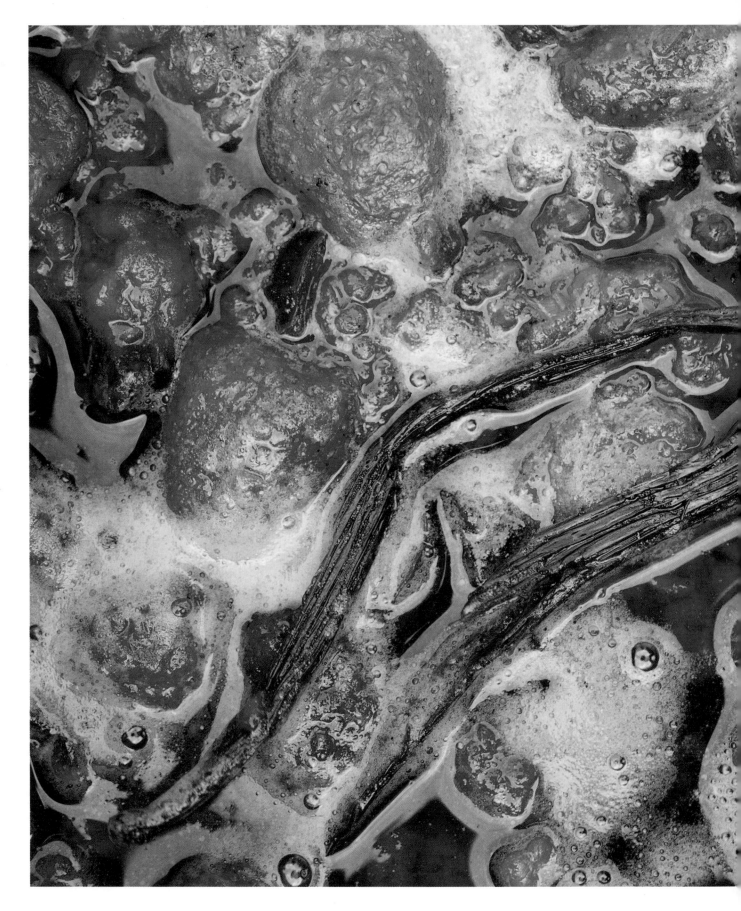

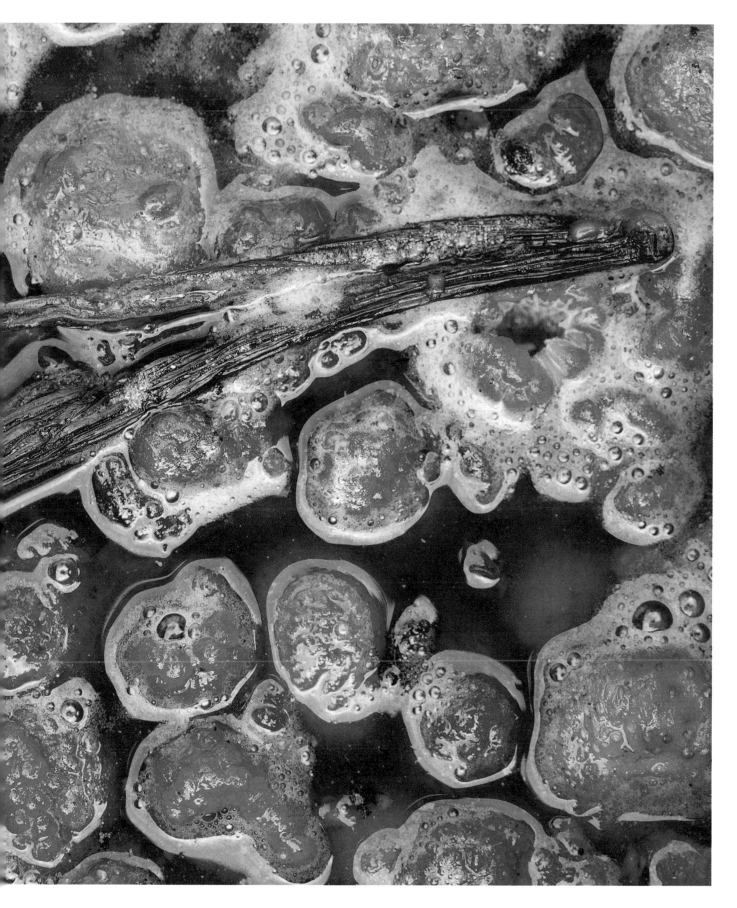

SWEETS AND TREATS

maple-tossed beluga lentil salad 107

berries

    classic berry smoothie 197

    cold red berry soup with cream 231

    flowered granola 51

    summer berry pancake cake 235

birch sugar *10*

black beans *8*

blackberries

    baked crunchy blackberry oatmeal 37

    chocolate & blackberry milkshake 186

black-eyed beans *8–9*

blueberries

    buckwheat & ginger porridge 57

    flour-free banana & coconut pancakes 45

borlotti beans 9

Brazil nuts 7

bread

    apple & mushroom-stuffed bread rolls 100

    dark Danish rye bread 58

breakfast blend 46

broad beans

    hash pan with broad beans 129

broccoli

    broccoli pesto 175

    broccoli salad with pomegranate & raisins 68

    wake-up smoothie 197

buckwheat, hulled 8

    buckwheat & ginger porridge 57

buns, cardamom & apple 208

burgers, portobello & peach 118

butter 7

    ghee (clarified butter) 25

    see also nut butters; seed butters

butter beans 9

butternut squash

    rhubarb, apple & yellow split pea stew 116

C

cabbage

    baked herb & pistachio falafel 65

    savoury tacos with corn & mango filling 82

    tom kha tofu 66

cabbage, red

    wild rice, artichoke & grape salad 76

cacao powder & nibs *12*

cakes

    cardamom & apple buns 208

    carrot, coconut & banana cupcakes 213

    decadent beetroot & chocolate cake 210

    double chocolate raspberry brownie 217

cakes (patties)

    quinoa, cauliflower & ramsons cakes 71

cakes, savoury

    savoury corn & millet muffins 95

cannellini beans 9

    mascarpone beanotto with oyster mushrooms
      & spinach 146

cardamom & apple buns 208

carob powder *12*

carrots

    carrot, coconut & banana cupcakes 213

    carrot & grapefruit juice 193

cashew nuts 7

    cashew & tomato dressing 131

    cashew nut dressing 65

    raw sour cream sauce 82

cauliflower

    pizza with a cauliflower base 86

    quinoa, cauliflower & ramsons cakes 71

    sweet apricot & cauliflower dal 115

ceviche

    sprout ceviche 167

chai

    sweet hazelnut masala chai 194

flour-free banana & coconut pancakes 45

Sicilian parmigiana di zucchine 136

see also frittata; omelettes

elderflower lemonade 203

F

falafels

baked herb & pistachio falafel 65

fennel

fennel & coconut tart 96

green cleanse power shot 193

lemony fennel & lentil salad 84

fermented essentials *13*

feta cheese

quinoa, cauliflower & ramsons cakes 71

savoury corn & millet muffins 95

fig, rhubarb & pear compôte 160

fillings

apple & mushroom filling 100

corn & mango filling 82

orange quinoa filling 98

purple beetroot filling 98

flax oil 7

flaxseeds *8*

flours *11*

frittata, herb & asparagus 38

frosting & icing

chocolate topping 217

cream cheese frosting 213

fruit

buckwheat & ginger porridge 57

fruit roll-ups 222

juicing 188

stone fruit salad with creamy goat's cheese 40

see also berries

G

gazpacho, strawberry 108

ghee (clarified butter) 7, 25

ginger, pickled 132

goat's cheese

beetroot, apple & goat's cheese wraps 98

green courgette topping 143

lemony fennel & lentil salad 84

stone fruit salad with creamy goat's cheese 40

white potato topping 143

goat's milk 9

goji *12*

grains *11*

sprouting 28

granitas

cantaloupe granita with lemon & mint 225

granola, flowered 51

grapefruit

carrot & grapefruit juice 193

grapes

wild rice, artichoke & grape salad 76

guacamole 118

H

halloumi cheese

amaranth & halloumi-stuffed tomatoes 152

haricot beans 9

hash pan with broad beans 129

hazelnut milk

sweet hazelnut masala chai 194

hazelnuts *8*

broccoli pesto 175

hazelnut, aubergine & mushroom parcels 126

hemp milk 9

hemp protein powder *12*

hemp seeds *8*

TACK. TAK. THANK YOU!

Elsa – you can't read this just yet but you have been stirring the bowls, playing in the grass and running around our legs while we have been trying recipes and taking the photos for this book. If you hadn't been such a miraculously happy child, we would never have landed this project on such a tight schedule. Maybe you will pick this book up 10 years from now and read this. You probably won't remember it, but you were part of this project. We love you.

Johanna – all the photos in the book are wonderful! It's not always easy to work with your brother, but you did an amazing job balancing on tables and patiently waiting for the perfect light. We are such big fans of your work and really happy that you wanted to be our photographer.

Kate and Chris – we had no idea how to do a cookbook. Thank you for holding our hands throughout this process. And for believing in us and staying positive through all our concerns and doubts.

To all our family in Denmark and Sweden – we can't thank you enough for your loving support and for helping us out with everything from trying a rye bread recipe or loaning your car, to teaching us how to roll a cinnamon bun like Grandma.

Affe and Marie, Erik and Hanna, Kristina, Stefan and Inga, and Anders – thank you for lending your summer houses to us while we worked on this book. Your houses, gardens, furniture, tableware and doors (!) made amazing settings and backgrounds for our photos. Plus, we had a great time there.

And to all our amazing blog readers. It is your constant support, constructive recipe feedback and cheering comments that motivate us to grow and improve our kitchen skills. Some of you also helped us testing the recipes in this book. A big thank you to (hope we haven't forgotten anyone now): Katie Dalebout, Jacquelyn Scoggin, Emily Meagher, Wendy Kastner, Line Sander Johansen, Elizabeth Allen, Michealla Redeker, Marijke Fisser, Matt & Amalie, Rikke Bülow Mindegaard Christensen, Natalia Mrukowicz, Susanne Irmer, Lisa Frenkel, Lydia Loeskow Söderberg, Helena Strand, Shadya Ghemati, Michèle Janse van Rensburg, Dana Slatkin, Yasmin Mckenzie, Anna Hastie, Blaine Tacker, Hjørdis Petersen, Jeanine Donofrio, Laura Gates, Sasha Gora, Modini Therese Natland, Sophie Pronovost, Klelia Shoo-Kara, Meg Pell, Benedikte Capion, Nicola Griffiths and Eveline Johnsson. Tack. Tak. Thank you!

ABOUT THE AUTHORS

David Frenkiel and Luise Vindahl are the couple
behind the critically acclaimed vegetarian food blog
Green Kitchen Stories, which has followers from
all over the world. Healthy, seasonal and delicious
vegetarian recipes paired with colourful and beautiful
photos have become a trademark of their style.
Their work has appeared in *Saveur, Bon Appetit,
Gourmet, Cook Vegetarian, ELLE, Babble* and *Jamie
Oliver's Food Revolution*. Their app 'Green Kitchen' was
selected as App of the Year Runner-Up in App Store
Best of 2012.
David is Swedish and Luise is Danish, and they
currently live in Stockholm with their daughter Elsa.
Apart from doing freelance recipe development and
photographing, David works as a magazine art director
and Luise is studying to become a nutritional therapist.
This is their first cookbook.

www.greenkitchenstories.com

The Green Kitchen by David Frenkiel & Luise Vindahl

First published in 2013 by Hardie Grant Books

Hardie Grant Books (UK)
Dudley House, North Suite
34–35 Southampton Street
London WC2E 7HF
www.hardiegrant.co.uk

Hardie Grant Books (Australia)
Ground Floor, Building 1
658 Church Street
Melbourne, VIC 3121
www.hardiegrant.com.au

British Library Cataloguing-in-Publication Data. A catalogue record
for this book is available from the British Library.

ISBN 978-1-74270-558-3

Commissioning Editor: Kate Pollard
Art Direction and design: Charlotte Heal
Photography and retouching: Johanna Frenkel
Colour reproduction by p2d

Printed and bound China by 1010 Printing International Limited

10 9 8 7